Hist
972.9064
B894m

DISCARDED BY
MEMPHIS PUBLIC LIBRARY

MAIN LIBRARY
Memphis and Shelby
County Public Library and
Information Center

For the Residents
of
Memphis and Shelby County

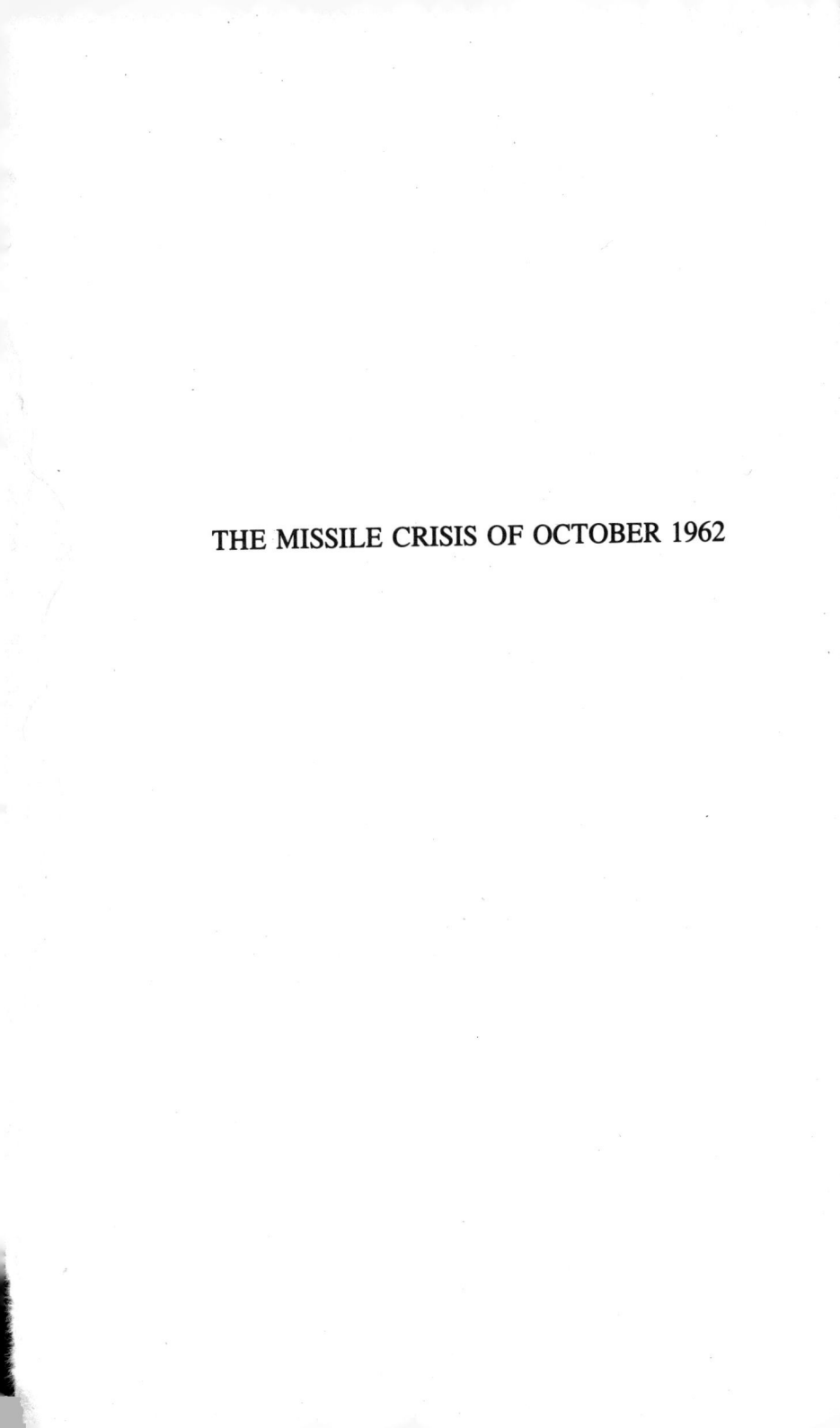

THE MISSILE CRISIS OF OCTOBER 1962

Guides to Historical Issues

Richard Dean Burns, Editor

#1 Who First Discovered America? A Critique of Writings on Pre—Columbian Voyages

EUGENE R. FINGERHUT

#2 The Missile Crisis of October 1962: A Review of Issues and References

LESTER H. BRUNE

THE MISSILE CRISIS OF OCTOBER 1962

A Review of Issues and References

LESTER H. BRUNE

REGINA BOOKS
Claremont, California

Copyright © 1985 by Lester H. Brune

All rights reserved.
This book or any part thereof may not be reproduced in any form without permission of the publisher.

Library of Congress Cataloging in Publication Data

Brune, Lester H.

   The missile crisis of October 1962.

   (Guides to historical issues ; #2)
   Bibliography: p.
   Includes index.
   1. Cuban Missile Crisis, Oct. 1962. I. Title. II Series.
E841.B78   1985   972.9.'064   85-14336

ISBN 0-941690-16-4
ISBN 0-941690-17-2 (pbk.)

Cover by Clinton Wade Graphic Design

Regina Books
Box 280
Claremont, CA 91711
Manufactured in the United States of America

Chronology

1 January 1959	Cuba's President Batista resigns; Castro's Revolutionary forces gain control of Cuba.
15 April 1959	U.S.–Cuban discussion on economic relations begin.
11 January 1960	U.S. ambassador protests Cuban seizure of American property.
11 July 1960	Soviet Chairman Khrushchev offers "rocket" support to Cuba.
19 October 1960	U.S. embargoes all exports to Cuba excepting medicine and food.
3 January 1961	U.S. severs diplomatic relations with Cuba.
13 February 1961	Soviet–Cuban trade agreement completed.
17–20 April 1961	Bay of Pigs invasion by Cuban exiles fails.
1 May 1961	Castro announces he is a socialist.
21 October 1961	U.S. indicates its superiority in nuclear weapons; there is no missile gap with the U.S.S.R.
27 July 1962	Castro indicates Cuba will soon have new defenses against the U.S.
29 August 1962	U–2 photos verify SAM defense missiles in Cuba.
4–13 September 1962	Kennedy "warns" Moscow not to place offensive missiles in Cuba.

14 October 1962	U−2 photos disclose MRBM and IRBM launch pads under construction in Cuba.
16 October 1962	First two secret sessions of ExCom to advise Kennedy on a U.S. response.
22 October 1962	JFK's speech informs the U.S. public of the Soviet missiles and announces a "naval quarantine" of Cuba.
24 October 1962	Soviet ships acknowledge the U.S. blockade.
26−27 October 1962	Washington receives two letters from Moscow regarding a "deal" for removing Soviet missiles.
27 October 1962	U−2 shot down in Cuba; Kennedy sends Krushchev a proposal to resolve the crisis.
28 October 1962	Khrushchev agrees to remove Soviet missiles and accepts Kennedy's pledge not to invade Cuba.
20 November 1962	U.S. announces removal from Cuba of the last Soviet missiles.

Preface

The Cuban missile crisis has inspired extensive investigation because it was the first "nuclear confrontation" between the United States and the Soviet Union. The present study examines a variety of analytical studies by scholars from various disciplines in order to reconstruct the crisis and to explain the major issues surrounding the decisions made in Moscow and Washington which led to the Soviet attempt to establish a missile base in Cuba, caused a U.S.–U.S.S.R. confrontation and, eventually, led to a common solution.

Scholars of the crisis have greater access to documents, memoirs and official papers from American sources than from Soviet sources. Nevertheless, analysts of Soviet behavior have developed methods which provide at least rudimentary insights into the Soviet decision process. While these scholars recognize the limitations of their estimates of Soviet policymaking, in the absence of more complete information, their methods provide a more informed means for evaluating Soviet activity than the biased assumptions of ideologues who place all blame on American imperialism or Soviet communism.

If deterrence nuclear policy is to succeed over the long term––a policy which presently appears to be the most practical means to avoid nuclear war––both American and Soviet decision–makers can profit from the analysis of the behavior of each other during crises. This requires a thorough study of the mistakes and successes leading to and, later, away from the brink of a nuclear holocaust in October 1962.

Twenty years after the Cuban crisis, the nuclear destructive capabilities available to two superpowers make intelligent analysis for deterring nuclear war more essential than ever before. The author hopes this summation of the October 1962 crisis, together with bibliographical references which may provide a detailed study of the crisis, will add to an understanding of the Cuban crisis: how it began, how it escalated, how it was resolved, and how it might have been better handled.

In preparing this study, the author incurred debts to many persons whose assistance or advice were essential. Richard Dean Burns suggested that the time was right for a recapitulation of our knowledge of the Cuban missile crisis. In addition, his encouragement and editorial direction has been indispensable. At Bradley University, a number of staff members made the production of this volume possible. The essential typing work was performed by Marian Phelps, Patricia Schramek and Lisa Crumley. Assisting in the final computer preparations were

Donald Raeuber, Evanne Dorethy and Kathy Lipovac. Without the efforts of these people, this volume would not have been possible. The contribution of each of the above persons is greatly appreciated.

>Lester H. Brune
>Bradley University

Contents

Chronology / v
Preface / vii
Introduction / 1

CHAPTER 1 **United States – Cuban Tensions, 1959-1962** / 4
Castro Gains Power In Cuba / 4
Castro, Khrushchev, and Kennedy: 1960 Election / 6
The Bay of Pigs / 9

CHAPTER 2 **The Soviet Decision to Place Missiles in Cuba** / 15
European Considerations / 17
Sino-Soviet Considerations / 19
The "Missile Gap" and Soviet Desire For Parity / 21
Khrushchev and Castro / 25
Khrushchev's Escalation of Aid to Cuba, 1960-1962 / 27

CHAPTER 3 **U.S. Detects Soviet Missiles, Aug. 29-Oct. 21** / 33
Domestic Politics and the Cuban Crisis / 33
Delay in Discovery of Offensive Missiles / 38
JFK's Search for Appropriate Response, Oct. 16-21 / 43
    Soviet Motives Assessed / 44
    Political-Diplomatic Considerations / 45
    Military Options Considered / 47
    The Blockade Decision / 51

CHAPTER 4 **JFK's Blockade Strategy, Oct. 22-28** / 55
Preparations to Announce the Blockade / 55
Blockade Increases Soviet-American Tensions / 57
    Monday: October 22 / 58
    Tuesday: October 23 / 60
    Wednesday to Friday Morning: October 24-26 / 62
    Friday Afternoon: October 26 / 65
    Saturday: October 27 / 67
Khrushchev Yields, October 28 / 70
Castro Objects to Withdrawal, Oct. 28-Nov. 20 / 71

CHAPTER 5 **Summary and Analysis** / 75
Kennedy and Khrushchev Claim Victory / 75
Soviet Miscalculations / 76
The October 26 and 27 Letters / 79

CHAPTER 6 **References / 83**
    Analytical and Historical Studies / 83
        A. General Surveys / 84
        B. Some Contemporary Account / 86
        C. Domestic American Politics / 90
        D. "Missile-Gap" Issues / 91
        E. Intelligence Operations: CIA and U-2 / 92
        F. U.S. Missiles in Turkey / 95
        G. Cuban "Blockade" and International Law / 96
        H. United Nations Role / 97
        I. OAS Activity / 98
        J. Canada and the Crisis / 99
        K. Europe and the Crisis / 99
        L. Documents on the Crisis / 101
    Participants in the 1962 Crisis / 104
        M. Americans / 104
            John F. Kennedy / 104
            Robert Kennedy / 109
            Dean Rusk / 109
            Adlai Stevenson / 110
            Other Americans / 111
        N. The Soviet Union / 113
            Nikita Khrushchev / 113
            Other Russians / 115
        O. Cubans / 115
    National Dimensions / 117
        P. The Soviet Dimension / 117
            Soviet Policy Making in the Crisis / 117
            Soviet-Cuban Relations / 120
            Sino-Soviet Relations and the Crisis / 121
        Q. The Cuban Dimension / 122
            United States, Cuba and the Caribbean / 122
            The United States and Castro / 124
            Kennedy, the CIA and Castro / 125
            Bay of Pigs Episode / 126
    National Security Dimensions / 127
        R. Deterrence Theory / 127
            General Deterrence Studies / 127
            Deterrence Studies on the 1962 Crisis / 129
            Leader Behavior and the Decision Process / 130

  S. Consequences of the Cuban Crisis / 133
    Detente and Arms Control / 133
    Renewed Military Build-up / 136
    Search for a Better Way to Handle a Crisis / 137
    The Kennedy-Khrushchev Understanding / 139
Basic References / 140
  T. Bibliographical and Archival Sources / 140
    Bibliographies / 140
    Archival Sources / 142
Author Index / 144

MAPS
  Locations of Offensive Missile Sites in Cuba / 34
  Range of Soviet Missiles / 56

Photo Courtesy of John F. Kennedy Library

Executive Committee of the National Security Council (ExCom)

Introduction

The Cuban Missile Crisis of 1962 brought the United States and the Soviet Union to the brink of nuclear war. To have been to the brink of a nuclear holocaust and to have avoided the conflict has several advantages. First and foremost, this event made American and Soviet leaders realize that nuclear war was a real possibility. In addition, the crisis provides analysts with an opportunity to study decision–making processes which first caused, and later enabled the two powers to resolve, the crisis.

This study seeks to assist in the understanding of the October 1962 decisions by describing how and why they were made. Chapters 1 through 5 present a brief narrative of the characters, issues and interpretations of the crisis, based on up–to–date research studies. Chapter 6 offers an extended bibliographical essay on the writings of the past twenty–two years which contributed to this narrative and analysis.

Students of the missile crisis have focused on several points; however, the following themes appear to encompass the most instructive issues.

Kennedy's Pre–crisis Policies. A historical crisis is seldom an accident of the moment. Following his election in 1960, President John F. Kennedy used confrontational cold war tactics which revised Dwight D. Eisenhower's efforts to establish "peaceful coexistence" with the Soviet Union. Not only in the Bay of Pigs incident of April 1961, but in the Congo, Berlin, and Vietnam, Kennedy undertook strong action to counter what he perceived as Soviet expansionism. He also began a build–up of America's armed forces to retain U.S. superiority. How did Kennedy's shift in U.S. policies and attitudes toward the Soviets and Cuba influence policy in Moscow and Havana as well as Washington, D.C.?

Soviet Miscalculations of American Behavior. Leaders of opposing nations cannot behave as "rational actors" before or during a crisis, unless they understand their differing political systems. What do the Soviets need to learn about such factors as U.S. political attitudes before a national election, the ability of the CIA to discover Cuban missile construction, and the U.S. perception of threat? In addition, why did the U.S. perceive "offensive" and "defensive" weapons differently than the Soviets?

American Decisions and American Politics. American politicians function in a domestic atmosphere of high visibility and high political vulnerability. Americans seem to prefer strong leaders and to dislike compromise or negotiation with communism. Why did Republicans, such as Senator Kenneth Keating, exaggerate the Cuban threat before the missile bases were discovered? Why would Kennedy's restrained response in September nearly cause him to order a secret attack on Cuba in October?

Gauging Soviet Intentions and Reactions. During the October crisis, Kennedy limited most of his consultations to ExCom (Executive Committee of the National Security Council) members. He did not consult widely with other advisors in the State or Defense Departments, or with scholars who disagreed with Kennedy's cold war ideas. Important questions must be raised regarding who was and who was not consulted. For the October crisis of 1962, how broad were the president's contacts with experts on Soviet behavior? with scholars of deterrence theory? with advocates of better relations with Cuba? and with proponents of a diplomatic solution to Cold War incidents?

Kennedy's Relations with Congress and Allies. In such instances as the Greek–Turkish crisis of February 1947 and the French crisis in Vietnam in April 1954, Presidents Truman and Eisenhower found advantages in consulting European allies and seeking bipartisan aid from congressional leaders. During the October 1962 crisis, Kennedy avoided such consultation, only informing Congress and American allies of his decisions on October 22 and expecting them to concur. Why did Kennedy avoid outside consultation? How did his decisions portend possible grave effects for both the NATO and OAS allies of the United States?

Advantages and Disadvantages of Kennedy's Public Announcement on October 22. Having decided on a naval quarantine of Cuba, President Kennedy announced the discovery of the Soviet missiles and his quarantine to a nationwide television audience. Subsequently, the critical decisions on war and peace were left to Khrushchev. The Soviets could seek to break the blockade, find another means to supply Cuba, or seek a face–saving deal which the U.S. might accept. Private negotiations were foreclosed. Was Kennedy's method designed to solve or to escalate the crisis? Did Kennedy's or Khrushchev's decisions become more crucial after the public announcement?

Kennedy's "Flexibility" vs. "Toughness". Immediately after the 1962 crisis ended, the public perception, encouraged by Kennedy's apologists, was that the president's "toughness" and America's military superiority assured his victory over Khrushchev. Later analysts denied this, indicating that both in choosing the quarantine and in avoiding war on Saturday, October 27, the president's flexibility was the critical characteristic which allowed Khrushchev to "save face" while agreeing to remove the Cuban missiles. In the outcome of the crisis, what were the relative merits of Kennedy's decisions between October 16 and 28, of U.S. military strength, and of the geographic location of Cuba? Was the quarantine a flexible or tough policy?

Deterrence Theory and the Cuban Crisis. After both the United States and the Soviet Union obtained thermonuclear weapons, and the intercontinental missiles to deliver these war heads to all parts of the world, intellectuals in many nations had to consider methods to avoid a nuclear holocaust. Deterring these two opponents or other nations with a potential nuclear capability became a necessity. While deterrence studies could examine other international crises to discover how war came about, the Cuba crisis of 1962 became the crisis best representing the actual threat of a nuclear exchange. For deterrence theory, all the previous questions raised in this introduction were parts of the larger questions: How can nuclear powers avoid reaching the point of nuclear confrontation? Should a crisis arise, what precautions should be taken to assure that neither side panics and orders an attack? What can be learned from the 1962 crisis about how the nuclear powers got into the crisis and how they avoided a nuclear war?

I

United States—Cuban Tensions, 1959–1962

Fidel Castro's triumphant march into Santiago on January 8, 1959, completed Cuba's revolutionary war. Fulgencia Batista had fled into exile on January 1. A year later, on January 11, U.S. Ambassador Philip W. Bonsal protested Castro's confiscation of American-owned property and Cuba's failure "to recognize the legal rights of U.S. citizens who have made investments in Cuba." United States efforts to negotiate with Castro had been controversial and, ultimately, futile. The disputes which had arisen in 1959 between Havana and Washington became caught up in the tensions between the Soviet Union and the United States when Nikita Khrushchev began to support Castro's cause. Within thirty months, the Moscow—Havana connection transformed Cuba into a Soviet base and brought the United States and the Soviet Union to the brink of a nuclear holocaust.

CASTRO GAINS POWER IN CUBA

In part, the 1962 missile crisis was rooted in America's inability to promote the successful evolution of a democratic government in Cuba. After relinquishing its controls under the Platt Amendment in 1934, Washington's economic and political interests in this nearby island prevented Cuba from evolving a government which attended to the needs of its populace. Emphasizing order, rather than freedom or independence, U.S. policy from Franklin D. Roosevelt to Dwight D. Eisenhower undertook to indirectly control Cuba's development. Thus, after 1953, the U.S. became associated with Batista's military dictatorship, a regime characterized by corruption, internal dissent, and repressive methods.

As guerrilla warfare increased in Cuba, the U.S. reluctantly dropped its support of Batista but failed to promote a suitable replacement.

Between 1955 and 1958, the Eisenhower administration did not actively assist the rebellion led by Fidel Castro but hoped that American newsmen were correctly assessing Castro's democratic aims. On February 24, 1957, Herbert Matthews began a series of articles in the *New York Times* which set the tone for U.S. news reports on Castro during the next two years. Following a visit with Castro at his Sierra Maestra mountain quarters, Matthews described Castro as "a man of ideals, of courage and of remarkable qualities of leadership." He reported that Castro's July 26th movement was nationalist and anticolonial. Castro, moreover, showed "no animosity toward the American people." He was "fighting for a democratic Cuba and an end to dictatorship."[1]

Arthur Gardner and Earl Smith, the last two American ambassadors to Cuba under Batista, later told a Congressional committee that American newsmen had greatly assisted Castro's victory. They insisted that the news media gave Castro a stature and backing he never deserved. Moreover, they argued, American congressmen and the State Department's Latin American desk had been persuaded by news reports to forsake Batista and favor Castro. Smith's book, *The Fourth Floor* (C-6), claimed that the State Department's sympathy toward Castro undermined Batista's government.[2]

While Gardner and Smith's strong predilection for Batista diluted their assessment of Castro's victory, moderate reporters such as Theodore Draper (O-4) and Hugh Thomas (Q-13) concluded that no one before 1959 could have predicted what Castro would do once in office. In their view, Castro made many promises such as land reforms and elections, which he never kept. Desiring to maintain his position as *Lider Maximo* after 1959, Castro acted as had many previous Latin American dictators, with but one difference: instead of relying on the United States for assistance in 1959, he turned to the Soviet Union where Khrushchev greeted him with open arms.[3]

Khrushchev welcomed Castro even though professional communists in Cuba's Communist Party (*Partido Socialista Popular* — PSP), had not accepted Castro as an orthodox disciple. Because he was an anti-American Third World leader who desired to improve Cuba's social and economic status, the Kremlin encouraged Castro by offering him money and military aid. They also offered a market for the Cuban sugar embargoed by the U.S., even though the Soviet Union had enough sugar for its domestic needs.

Although Castro distrusted the Moscow-oriented PSP and separated his party — the United Party of the Socialist Revolution — from the

PSP leadership, the Cuban leader gained sympathy from both Red China and the Soviet Union. While Mao Tse–tung's beliefs were probably dearer to Castro's heart, only Khrushchev could offer the economic and military aid Castro needed to fend off America. Consequently, after the negotiations between Cuba and Washington floundered in 1959, Anastas Mikoyan, the Soviet Deputy Prime Minister, visited Cuba on February 13, 1960, and signed a commercial agreement to purchase Cuban sugar.[4]

Castro did not announce his communist beliefs until December 1961. Yet, many Americans, including Washington leadership, became readily convinced that Castro had duped them prior to 1959, by advocating free elections, freedom and capitalist virtues. In addition, many non–communist groups in Cuba opposed Castro, but they were too factionalized to supplant the new leader whose charisma rallied the peasant–worker populace to his standard. Early in 1959, for example, Castro named David Salvador, the labor leader of the 26th of July Movement, as the Secretary General of the Cuban Confederation of Labor (CTC). During the Confederation's National Congress meeting in November, Salvador fell from Castro's grace. Appearing before the Congress, Fidel accused the labor delegates of disunity. He replaced its leaders with a three–member board, including the pro–Communist, Jesus Soto. Salvador ended up in prison and the labor confederation became subservient to the Ministry of Labor, having lost its bargaining power.[5]

Between 1959 and 1961, Castro became closely associated with the Soviet Union. In addition to sending military and economic aid, Khrushchev, on July 11, 1960, threatened America with a nuclear attack if it tried to intervene in Cuba. He told a Soviet teacher's convention that "in case of necessity, Soviet artillery men can support the Cuban people with their rocket fire."[6] Not surprisingly, therefore, the U.S.–Cuban–Soviet tensions became a key foreign policy issue during the 1960 presidential campaign.

CASTRO, KHRUSHCHEV, AND KENNEDY'S 1960 ELECTION

Domestic and personality issues, however, largely dominated the 1960 presidential campaign between John F. Kennedy and Richard Nixon. Insofar as foreign policy issues entered the political debates, the Democrats criticized the previous Republican administration for creating a "missile gap" which would soon give the Soviets nuclear superiority, and for permitting Cuba to slip into the communist orbit.

In Soviet relations and U.S. national security affairs, Eisenhower's policies had attempted to relieve tensions with Moscow, strengthen European defenses, and design a U.S. defense posture geared to a long-haul Cold War struggle. He sought to accomplish all this without jeopardizing America's economic prosperity. The Republican president found Khrushchev, Stalin's successor, willing to seek an era of "peaceful coexistence." Until the U-2 crisis of May 1960, the effort to moderate tensions seemed successful. However for many U.S. Cold War warriors, including Senator John F. Kennedy, Eisenhower's establishment of a friendly "spirit of Camp David" with Khrushchev in 1959, and the president's unwillingness to promote huge defense expenditures were characterized as "softness" toward the communist menace.

Criticism against Eisenhower's "new look" defense policy began in 1957, and was enhanced by two Soviet successes which were interpreted as giving the Soviet Union technological leadership over America. In August, Moscow launched an intercontinental ballistic missile (ICBM) capable of reaching American targets from Soviet territory. More dramatically, in October, the Soviets placed the first earth satellite, *Sputnik*, into an orbit where it passed regularly over the United States.

Responding to the shock of fear generated amidst the American public by *Sputnik*, Senator Kennedy denounced Eisenhower for allowing the Soviet Union the possibility of achieving nuclear superiority. In a Senate address on August 14, 1958, Kennedy used data from such defense advocates as Henry A. Kissinger to claim that there would be a "missile gap" between 1960 and 1964, which "would in all likelihood be weighted heavily against us." While the Soviets would thus be able to launch a surprise nuclear attack, more probably, they would "use their superior striking ability to achieve their objectives in ways which may not require launching an actual attack." Behind their nuclear superiority, they could use "sputnik diplomacy" — intimidation, subversion, and blackmail to advance their world domination. "The periphery of the free world will slowly be nibbled away. The balance of power will gradually shift against us."[7]

As Richard Aliano (D-1) indicates, Kennedy exploited post-Sputnik fears to gain the Executive Mansion. He used the missile-gap thesis to secure support from the military-industrial establishment which opposed Eisenhower's attempt to stabilize the growing defense costs by cutting funds of the nation's conventional armed forces. (The missile gap issue shall be developed later because it influenced both Kennedy's and Khrushchev's policies during the year preceding the 1962 missile crisis.)

In addition to the missile gap, Eisenhower's alleged "loss of Cuba" became a Democratic campaign weapon during the 1960 election. According to historian Kent Beck (C−1), Kennedy's political advisors decided in 1960 that Cuba was an ideal symbol of "American decline under Eisenhower." Thus, Kennedy frequently told voters: "In 1952, the Republicans ran on a program of rolling back the Iron Curtain in Eastern Europe. Today, the Iron Curtain is 90 miles off the coast of the United States." On October 6, in a Cincinnati speech, Kennedy went further, calling Cuba "the most glaring failure of American foreign policy today," and asserting "it was our own policies — not Castro's — that first began to turn our former good neighbors against us."[8]

Vice President Richard M. Nixon, the Republican presidential nominee in 1960, struggled to defend Eisenhower's policies without disclosing the secret information he had regarding the president's order to the CIA to train Cuban exiles for a possible return to their homeland. Thus, he reacted to Kennedy's October 6 speech by claiming, "Cuba is not lost...." The United States, he said, was applying economic pressure against Castro. Moreover, the "free people of Cuba, the people who want to be free, are going to be supported and...they will attain their freedom."

Kennedy's Cuban campaign rhetoric peaked on October 20−21, just before and during the final Nixon−Kennedy television debate. On October 20, Kennedy's advisors released a position paper on Cuba which advocated diplomatic action in the Organization of American States (OAS), strong U.S. economic sanctions, aid to Latin America, and assistance for the "non−Batista democratic anti−Castro forces in exile and in Cuba itself...." The last proposal enraged Nixon when the *New York Times* emphasized it with the headline, "Kennedy Advocated U.S. Intervention in Cuba."[9]

Nixon believed Kennedy violated the conditions under which he received classified data about Eisenhower's aid to Cuban exiles. Nevertheless, during and after the October 21 debate, Nixon attacked Kennedy's proposal as "dangerously irresponsible" on two counts: it suggested that the U.S. should violate treaties with Latin American nations and the United Nations; and, second, it invited Khrushchev to intervene in Cuba.[10]

The political rhetoric of the 1960 election, combined with Eisenhower's July 6 announcement that Cuba's sugar quota was being cut by ninety-five percent, resulted in increased tension between the U.S. and its island neighbor. During the fall of 1960, Castro nationalized 382 private firms and assumed control of all banks and sugar mills. In retaliation, the U.S. requested an indictment of Castro in the United Nations General Assembly, embargoed all trade to Cuba and recalled its ambassador, Philip W. Bonsal. By October 1960, rumors were circulating about U.S. plots to overthrow Cuba. Fearing an impending U.S. attack, Castro's ties to the Soviet Union became his principal source for obtaining military equipment to protect his island. Khrushchev, as noted above, promised to use Soviet rockets to protect Cuba, and shipped "at least 28,000 tons" of weapons to Cuba, according to a State Department assertion of November 18. Castro welcomed Khrushchev's rocket pledge and viewed Soviet aid as a warning designed to deter an American invasion.

Following Kennedy's narrow victory over Nixon, Castro hoped the new president would be more amenable. On January 20, 1961, Castro declared he was willing to receive U.S. overtures to renew diplomatic relations, because he saw "a little hope...for peace" under Kennedy's presidency. Castro's hopes were in vain. On February 24, State Department spokesman Lincoln White contended U.S.-Cuban disputes would not end until Cubans could "freely choose their destiny." By that date, Kennedy had ordered the CIA to continue its planning of the Cuban exile's invasion of Cuba.[11]

THE BAY OF PIGS

Castro was hardly surprised when Cuban exiles, aided by the CIA, launched their counter-revolutionary invasion on April 15-17, 1961. On January 5, 1961, Cuban Foreign Minister Raul Roa told the United Nations Security Council that the U.S. was planning an "immediate" invasion by "mercenaries" being trained in Guatemala, Honduras, and Florida. The Security Council rejected Roa's charges, and refused to pass a resolution labeling the U.S. an aggressor against Cuba.

The Cuban leaders had heard, as had others in Southern Florida, that CIA preparations were underway to train anti-Castro Cubans for an invasion. Indeed, President Eisenhower had approved CIA training of exile groups in March 1960. On January 3, 1961, Eisenhower broke diplomatic relations with Cuba, leading Castro to anticipate a U.S.-backed invasion before Kennedy's inauguration. This attack did not take place but soon after becoming president, Kennedy secretly ordered the CIA to continue preparing for the exile invasion force.

Planning for the Cuban operation was led by CIA Director Allen Dulles and his assistant, Richard Bissell, both of whom had served the Eisenhower Administration. Together with General Lyman Lemnitzer, Chairman of the Joint Chiefs of Staff, and Admiral Arleigh Burke, Chief of Naval Operations, the CIA leaders assured Kennedy the operation would succeed even though, according to Peter Wyden's study (Q-34), a CIA report of January 30 stated that over thirty percent of Cuba's population supported Castro.

Although other intelligence data disputed the CIA's report, Kennedy decided not to cancel the preparations to assist the Cuban counter-revolutionaries. Historian Richard Walton (M-17) argues that if Kennedy's intentions had been otherwise, he could have stopped the operation between January 22 and 28, when he was briefed on the details of the operation. Kennedy did not give Bissell definite approval, but ordered continuation of preparations and a revision of plans in order to lessen the direct involvement of United States forces.

Between January 28 and April 5, the latter being the date originally set for the exile's landing, plans for the Cuban operation changed from guerrilla infiltration to an invasion. Under the direction of Bissell and General David W. Gray, who the Joint Chiefs assigned to oversee military operations, the plan to land near Trinidad was dropped in favor of a landing near the Zapata swamps. The CIA initially planned a dawn landing of Cuban Brigade 2506 near Trinidad, at the foot of the Escambray Mountains on Cuba's southeast coast. After the landing, the exiles would join Cuban guerrillas in the mountains, where they could launch an extended campaign on Castro's forces. On March 16, new plans given to the president anticipated a night landing near the Zapata swamps at Cochinos Bay (Bay of Pigs). One of the plan's most serious defects was that no Cuban guerrillas operated near Zapata. This location was selected as good for a night landing and because it had an aircraft runway; however, according to Wyden, no one at Kennedy's briefing emphasized the lack of nearby guerrilla support for the Brigade. The new plan did, however, fulfill one of Kennedy's principal criteria because it minimized the direct U.S. role in the operation. Bissell claimed U.S. troops were not essential because a popular Cuban uprising would begin if a bridgehead was created. Wyden attributes this fundamental misjudgment to Bissell's emotional commitment to the operation.

While the CIA trained, equipped and planned for the Bay of Pigs operation, the U.S. State Department on April 3 issued a Cuban "White Paper" which justified the exiles' efforts to eliminate Castro and restore "free institutions." Written by Arthur Schlesinger, Jr., the "White Paper" claimed Cuba's regime threatened the entire Western Hemisphere: "What began as a movement to enlarge Cuban democracy had been perverted, in short, into a mechanism for the destruction of free institutions in Cuba, for the seizure by international communism of a base and bridgehead to the Americas, and for the disruption of the inter-American System." Finally, the report encouraged the Cuban people to continue striving for a free Cuba.[12]

From its first hours on April 15, the Bay of Pigs episode was a fiasco. Hoping to destroy Castro's air power, eight B-26 bombers disguised as Cuban planes attacked Cuban air bases, including the main base at Camp Colombia. Subsequently, one B-26 crashed into the ocean near Cuba; a second landed unexpectedly near Key West, Florida, after being hit by Cuban anti-aircraft fire; and the remaining planes returned to their Guatemalan base to prepare for a second strike scheduled for the day of invasion, April 17.

The CIA's plans for the air attack did not succeed. Photos of the air raids disclosed that all Castro's planes had not been destroyed. At the same time, the CIA cover story for the air raids proved unsatisfactory. When the eight B-26's left Guatemala for Cuban targets, a ninth flew to Florida where the pilot was to land and announce that he had deserted Castro's forces and bombed the Cuban air fields. By Saturday afternoon, this "cover" story fell apart as two reports challenged the "deserter's" account. First, a B-26 which crashed into the ocean after attacking Cuba was found floating nearby. Secondly, the B-26 pilot who had landed his disabled plane near Key West was not mentioned in the CIA's cover story.

More seriously, the CIA did not anticipate that Cuba would go immediately to the United Nations. Castro knew, of course, that the desertion story was false. Joined by the Soviet Union's delegation, Cuba demanded a Saturday session of the U.N. Political Committee where Soviet Ambassador Valery A. Zorin and Cuba's Raul Roa accused the U.S. of active aggression. The bombing planes, they said, were not Cuban but the first stage of a large scale U.S.—backed invasion of Cuba.

As both Wyden and Schlesinger (M—5) agree, CIA secrecy permitted Adlai Stevenson, the American ambassador to the U.N., to obtain only a vague idea about "Operation Zapata." Subsequently, at the U.N. sessions, Stevenson could not respond with proper caution to the Soviet charges. Unwittingly, Stevenson repeated the fabrication devised by the CIA's cover story and broadcast from Florida. The U.S. was not involved, Stevenson argued, because the pilot who landed in Miami was a defector from the Cuban air force.

Before the day ended, news reports of the two disabled B—26s, as well as other disclosures, substantially contradicted the CIA cover story. First, Castro announced that rocket bomb fragments had been found with the marking "U.S.A." Secondly, an auxiliary fuel tank used to extend the flying range of the B—26's was found twelve miles off the coast of Havana. Finally, the Cuban Revolutionary Council in America said six planes, not three, had bombed bases in Cuba. Both Moscow and Peking radio broadcasts warned that they and "all peace—loving nations" would cooperate in preventing a successful American attack on Cuba. Chairman Khrushchev wrote to Kennedy, asking the president to halt the aggression.

Because of Saturday's disclosures, President Kennedy decided on Sunday, April 16, to cancel the second B—26 air strike scheduled for Monday morning when the amphibious invasion began at the Bay of Pigs. Kennedy contended that the Cuban affair must not upset the U.S.'s larger world interests. It was too late, however, to cancel the landing. The invasion fleet had left Guatemala; and since the exiles were anxious to proceed, the CIA did not believe it could afford to discourage them.

Early on Monday, April 17, the Bay of Pigs invasion began without the second air strike. The Saturday air raid had failed to knock out two B—26 bombers, four fighter planes and several T—33 jet trainers. Castro's remaining planes supported Cuba's 20,000 troops which, with tanks and artillery, encircled the landing beaches. The CIA's plan to overthrow Castro with 1,200 exile soldiers had little chance as the internal uprisings never materialized. Castro's forces easily captured those exiles who reached the beach.[13]

The Bay of Pigs disaster strengthened Castro's hold on Cuba. It also prompted Kennedy to reassert his claim that communism could not be permitted to survive in Cuba. Over national television, he told the

American Society of Newspaper Editors that "we do not intend to abandon" Cuba to communism. Depicting Cuba as "less a threat to our survival than it is a base for subverting the survival of other free nations in the Western hemisphere," Kennedy said that "if the nations of this hemisphere should fail to meet their commitments against outside communist penetration, then I want it clearly understood that this government will not hesitate in meeting its primary obligation" and "intervene if necessary."[14] As the division between the U.S. and Cuba became irreparable, the "friendship" between Castro and Khrushchev grew stronger. Throughout the remainder of 1961, the Soviet Union rushed conventional military, as well as economic, aid to Cuba.

NOTES

1. Herbert Matthews, *New York Times*, February 24, 25, and 26, 1957.

2. Testimony of Gardner and Smith in U.S. Senate, Subcommittee to Investigate the Administration of the Internal Security Act, *Communist Threat to the United States Throughout the Caribbean* (Washington, DC: G.P.O., 1960), Part IX, 665–667, 686–7; Earl T. Smith, *The Fourth Floor* (New York: Random House, 1962), *passim*.

3. Theodore Draper, *Castro's Revolution: Myths and Realities* (New York: Praeger, 1962), 115–172; Hugh Thomas, *Cuba, the Pursuit of Freedom* (New York: Harper & Row, 1971), 1194–1254.

4. Herbert Dinerstein, *The Making of a Missile Crisis* (Baltimore: Johns Hopkins University Press, 1976), 69–152.

5. Draper, *Castro's Revolution*, 25–26.

6. Dinerstein, *Making a Missile Crisis*, 40–111.

7. John F. Kennedy, *John Fitzgerald Kennedy: A Compilation of Statements and Speeches Made During His Service in the United States Senate and House of Representatives*, 88th Cong. 2nd Sess. Senate Document No. 79 (Washington, DC: G.P.O., 1964), 704–715.

8. Kent M. Beck, "Necessary Lies, Hidden Truths: Cuba in the 1960 Campaign," *Diplomatic History* 8 (Winter 1984), 45.

9. *Ibid.*, 47–51.

10. The texts of the debates are in Sidney Kraus', *The Great Debates, 1960* (Glouchester, MA: Peter Smith, 1968), 411–430.

11. For a survey of the events of the fall of 1960 and 1961, see *Cuba, The United States and Russia, 1960–1963* (New York: Facts on File, 1964), 30–40.

12. Arthur Schlesinger, Jr., *The Thousand Days* (New York: Houghton Mifflin, 1965), 232–266.

13. Peter Wyden, *Bay of Pigs: The Untold Story* (New York: Simon and Schuster, 1979), *passim*. For further details on the CIA role, see Lucien S. Vandenbroucke, "The Confessions of Allen Dulles: New Evidence on the Bay of Pigs," *Diplomatic History* 8 (Fall 1984), 365–375; and Richard M. Bissell, Jr., "Response to Lucien S. Vandenbroucke," *ibid.*, 377–380.

14. John F. Kennedy, *Public Papers of the Presidents: John F. Kennedy–1961* (Washington, DC: G.P.O., 1962), 304–306.

II

The Soviet Decision to Place Missiles in Cuba

During the first half of 1962, the Soviet Presidium decided to place medium (MRBM) and intermediate (IRBM) range ballistic missiles in Cuba. The decision not only changed the Soviet Union's previous policy of constructing nuclear missile sites only on Soviet soil, but also challenged America's position in the Western Hemisphere. The Soviet Union had greatly increased Cuba's supply of conventional weapons throughout 1961 with almost no complaints from the United States. The missile decision differed, however, because nuclear armed MRBMs and ICBMs in Cuba would be able to reach most U.S. cities as well as Central America and much of South America.

Since 1962, a variety of reasons have been advanced to explain Moscow's decision to place missiles in Cuba. Kennedy's apologists claimed that Khrushchev was testing the president's will; while Khrushchev and Castro both contended the missiles would protect Cuba from an American invasion or threat of invasion. Most analysts, however, have concluded that these two concepts are politically self−serving. While these analysts disagree on the precise reason for the Presidium's decision, their conclusions may be seen as parts of one general idea: Khrushchev's desire to gain a foreign policy success in one or all of the four areas in which he had suffered set backs between 1955 and 1962. These four areas were: Central Europe, China, Soviet nuclear weakness, and Moscow's ability to lead revolutions in the Third World.

According to Graham Allison (A−2), the earliest and most widely accepted explanation was that Khrushchev was testing Kennedy's and America's will to respond to an aggressive Soviet move. During the October 22, 1961 speech announcing the presence of Soviet missiles in Cuba, Kennedy stated that the Soviet missiles were a provocative, unjustified change in "the status quo, which cannot be accepted by this country if our courage and our commitment are ever to be trusted again by either friend or foe."[1] Following the crisis, Kennedy's two closest advisors, Arthur Schlesinger, Jr. (M−5) and Theodore Sorensen (M−7), promoted this theory and, its corollary, that Kennedy successfully demonstrated his will by standing firm to thwart Khrushchev's challenge.

Schlesinger provided the most explicit account of the "testing the will" concept when he wrote: "In a general sense, the decision [of Moscow] obviously represented the supreme Soviet probe of American intentions." According to Schlesinger, the Soviets believed Americans were "too rich," and "too soft," and "too liberal" to respond effectively to Moscow's "crucial test." President Kennedy, however, withstood the test. Thus, the thirteen days of October became Kennedy's, and thus America's, "finest hour" by meeting the communist threat.[2]

In contrast to Schlesinger, Ronald Steel (M−36) believes Kennedy saw himself being tested in the context of the upcoming November congressional elections and the 1964 presidential contest. As interpreted by Steel, Kennedy wanted a victory over Khrushchev to enhance his political prestige.

Roger Hilsman (M−55) disputes Steel's contention. Although Hilsman admits the crisis was a domestic political test for Kennedy, he contends the test was in terms of personal credibility with the U.S. military, the CIA, and State Department hard−liners. Hilsman says Kennedy had to stand tough to retain the respect of the Washington organizational bureaucrats. Later, extreme "hawks" such as General Max Johnson (B−12) and General LeMay denounced Kennedy for not ordering a massive attack to liberate Cuba from communism on October 27, if not on October 16.[3]

The transcript of the tape recording of Kennedy's October 16 meeting with his high−level advisors confirms that the president's advisors at that time did not consider the Soviet motives as a test of the president's will. The ExCom believed the Kremlin's motives were either to equalize the missile balance or secure gains in Berlin or Turkey. No one at the October 16 sessions suggested that Moscow was testing the will of the president or the American public.[4]

Subsequent to the missile crisis, most analysts rejected the idea that Khrushchev's gamble in Cuba was a "test." This rationale underestimated both Soviet planning and decision making. Scholars such as Horelick and Rush (P−6), and Weintal and Bartlett (A−10) contended that if Khrushchev desired to "test" Kennedy, he could have done so at a location more favorable to the Soviet Union, such as Berlin or

Turkey. Once the U.S. became aware of the Soviet base construction in Cuba, military conditions probably would favor the president. Consequently in Cuba the Soviets hoped to strengthen one of their weak outposts, but one that was clearly recognized as not vital to defending Russia. Also Soviet influence in Cuba was of potential, but not essential, value to Moscow. If necessary, the Kremlin could draw back from Cuba, as indeed Khrushchev did on October 28. Consequently, as Graham Allison concludes, it is not likely that the Soviets viewed the Cuban gamble as a "test" of Kennedy's decisiveness.[5]

More critical to Khrushchev than "testing" Kennedy's will was the Soviet leader's desire for a highly visible foreign policy victory. As Michael Tatu (P-14) explains in detail, Khrushchev was engaged in a power struggle in the Kremlin. Since 1957, both his domestic and foreign policies had gone awry. At the time of the Cuban crisis, Khrushchev sought a foreign policy triumph in one or more of four areas: (1) the European situation, (2) the Sino-Soviet split, (3) the search for nuclear parity with the U.S., and (4) the connection with Castro as a symbol of Moscow's leadership of national liberation movements.

EUROPEAN CONSIDERATIONS

Soviet leaders have consistently given their highest priority to "the defense of the revolution and homeland." As Stephen S. Kaplan has explained, the Soviets have remembered and acted in accordance with their fear that the Western European and American imperialists will invade their homeland as they did in 1914, from 1918 to 1920, and in 1941.

The activity of NATO forces during Eisenhower's Administration reinforced Moscow's fears. The United States had built up the NATO forces, rearmed West Germany and, in 1957, decided to deploy intermediate-range and submarine missile bases in NATO countries. The Soviet homeland would be threatened from the Arctic region of Norway through Central and Western Europe to Italy, Greece and Turkey in the Eastern Mediterranean.[6]

To counteract NATO decisions, the Warsaw Pact powers and Moscow first proposed the creation of a nuclear free zone in Central Europe. In 1957, Adam Rapacki, Poland's Foreign Minister, suggested the creation of a European nuclear-free zone. On March 3, 1958, the

Kremlin supported the Rapacki plan. As conceived, the zone would initially include Poland, Czechoslovakia and the two Germanies. No atomic, hydrogen or rocket weapons would be manufactured or deployed in this area. The Soviet Union referred to the creation of the zone as "the most pressing international problem calling for immediate solution."

The Western European nations and the U.S. may have rejected the Rapacki Plan too quickly. While the Western leaders claimed the zone would perpetuate the imbalance of East—West conventional forces in favor of the Communist block, Adam Ulam argues that, in the long—term, a nuclear—free Central Europe could benefit NATO once its European defense forces were established.

The Rapacki Plan was directly related to the larger Berlin issue which disturbed the Soviets and their Eastern European allies. From 1958 to 1962, Khrushchev endeavored to cajole the Western nations into settling the questions concerning the post—war division of Berlin and the establishment of Germany's boundaries. On November 10, 1958, Khrushchev declared the "occupation regime in Berlin" should end. He threatened to hand over Soviet power in Berlin to East Germany if the West refused to formalize an agreement within six months.

Eventually, Khrushchev withdrew his deadline and agreed to conduct foreign minister talks on Berlin. Until 1962, however, he continued to initiate many small irritating activities in Germany as American army convoys were halted and Western aircraft were buzzed in the Berlin air corridor. The German question was not answered to Khrushchev's satisfaction. Finally, on August 12—13, 1961, Soviet forces aided the East Germans in sealing off West Berlin by erecting the barricades which soon became the Berlin wall. Both sides made threatening gestures of force, but an East—West conflict was avoided.

By 1962, the East Germans were dismayed by Khrushchev's inability to resolve the status of divided Berlin. Michael Tatu indicates that various Moscow—Berlin communications between February and June 1962, indicated a developing friction between Walter Ulbricht, the communist head of East Germany, and Khrushchev. In February, Khrushchev promised Ulbricht that Moscow would "do something about the Berlin issue." Consequently, Tatu concludes that the objective of Khrushchev's gamble in Cuba "was clearly Berlin." Missiles in Cuba could strategically threaten Washington, D.C. and pressure Kennedy to yield on Berlin. If successful, Khrushchev could gain a strategic victory as well as a settlement on Berlin. Perhaps even the Soviet defenses in Central Europe would be improved.[7]

SINO–SOVIET CONSIDERATIONS

Khrushchev's second category of concern in 1962 was the Soviet dispute with the Chinese communist government, a split which became evident to the world in November 1961, and widened throughout 1962. Following Joseph Stalin's death in 1953, the People's Republic of China had become sufficiently independent to contest Russia's dominance of the international communist movement. Peking's demands for maintaining its loyalty to the Kremlin pushed the alliance to the breaking point in 1960. During an international communist conference at Bucharest, Rumania in June and a Moscow Conference in November, the differences between Khrushchev and Mao Tse–tung were debated within high communist circles. Although the non–communist world did not learn about these internal disputes until November 1961, leaders in Moscow and Peking realized that their outward show of communist solidarity was a facade for a dispute which could not easily be resolved.

Western scholars disagree about the exact reasons for the Sino–Soviet split. As British historian Edward Crankshaw indicates, the ideological dispute between Khrushchev and Mao about who most correctly interpreted Marx and Lenin was only the exterior rhetoric of deeper disagreements. The ideological differences reflected the more recent success of China's revolution, the historic antagonisms between the Russians and Chinese, and the nationalistic desires of the two divergent cultures. In specific terms, for the years from 1955 to 1962, the dispute focused on whether Mao or Khrushchev was the proper leader of the Third World revolutions, and on how "peaceful coexistence" should be pursued with the United States.

More significantly, as Adam Ulam emphasized, the split represented practical issues between Mao and Khrushchev. The Chinese wanted to obtain Soviet assistance in developing their own nuclear weapons, a wish the Kremlin would not fulfill. From Moscow's perspective, Soviet security would be in greater jeopardy if their eastern communist neighbor had nuclear weapons.[8]

During the 1960 Bucharest and Moscow meetings, Moscow and Peking debated their differences in terms of which international policies communists should follow. Because Peking had disputed Khrushchev's approach to peaceful coexistence from 1956 to 1960, the Soviet delegation at Bucharest gave representatives of each national group a circular letter defending Khrushchev against the Chinese criticisms. The letter argued that peaceful coexistence had enabled the communists to grow stronger as capitalism declined. It also noted that modern methods of warfare required changes, quoting Lenin as acknowledging that imperialists must sometimes be contested by peaceful methods. Finally, the Soviet letter blamed Mao for being incapable of recognizing, and acting according to, the changes in the balance of world forces.

After the Chinese delegate, Peng Chen, tried to counter Moscow's allegations, Khrushchev took the podium in Bucharest to attack the Chinese in violent terms which included personal criticism of Mao. Khrushchev denounced Mao as an "ultra−Leftist, an ultra−dogmatist, indeed, a left revisionist." The Chinese, he said, were "Trotskyites," attempting to force their beliefs on other communists.

During the November Moscow sessions, Khrushchev rallied all national communists parties except Albania to denounce Chinese concepts. Following the lead of delegate Tim Buck of Canada, various national delegates from Latin America, the Middle East and Africa arose to criticize Maoism. Only Enver Hoxha of Albania backed the Chinese delegate, Deng Xiaoping, in disputing Khrushchev's peaceful policies toward the imperialist world and his failure to support the cause of violent revolution as the best method for destroying capitalism. Concluding a speech which had denounced Khrushchev for dallying around the capitalist leaders rather than promoting communism, Deng defied the contention that all communists must follow Moscow's dictates. He asserted that: "In relations between parties there is no reason to demand that the minority should submit to the majority, for between parties there are no superiors and inferiors, each party is independent...." This, of course, was heresy to the Russians for, since 1919, Soviet leaders claimed to be the sole guide to international communist directions.

Throughout 1961, the Sino−Soviet split was generally hidden from the public. At the end of the Moscow conference, China signed the Moscow Declaration as a show of solidarity. Although Soviet technicians returned to China to assist their development programs, neither Mao nor Khrushchev actively sought to heal the breach. During November 1961, information about the communist split appeared in the western press when delegates to the two conferences from France, Italy and Belgium published their accounts of the 1960 events. The French communist leader, Maurice Thorez wrote: "We have not acquired the certitude that it is not a matter of disagreement limited to two or three points of the Declaration proposed at this [Moscow] conference, but of an entire line opposed to the international Communist movement....It is not a matter of divergences between the Chinese Communist Party and the Communist Party of the Soviet Union, but of a profound disagreement of the Chinese comrades with the whole international communist movement."[9]

By 1962, Khrushchev contended for communist leadership with the Chinese who, while in the minority, had challenged the Soviet leader on basic points of policy. One of the areas challenged by Maoism was the leadership of national liberation movements in the Third World. Cuba became one nation in which the Chinese hoped to supplant Moscow because Castro's ideas on peasant revolution correlated closely with Mao's notions. In 1962, however, China could not offer Cuba the economic and political prestige which the Soviet Union could use to counter America. To retain this advantage, however, the Kremlin had to prove it would act firmly and effectively in aiding national liberation movements. Thus, during the Cuban crisis, Khrushchev may have been challenging Peking as much as Washington.

THE "MISSILE–GAP" AND SOVIET DESIRE FOR PARITY

Between 1956 and 1962, the Soviet Union searched for some means to attain parity with the United States in strategic nuclear weapons. Since 1945, America's nuclear advantage had deterred the Soviets from overt or aggressive moves; in addition, it restricted the Kremlin to policies acceptable to the United States.

Following his 1957 success in the launching of Sputnik and the firing of an ICBM, Chairman Khrushchev often boasted that the U.S.S.R. could now unleash its big rockets on its enemies if necessary. According to Desmond Ball (D–2), in January 1961 the Soviets had operational ICBMs only at two test sites. In October 1962, an NSC study said the Soviets had about 10 operational ICBMs.

Khrushchev's pre–1960 boasts aided President Eisenhower's American opponents more than they served the Soviet Union's security interests. These critics of Eisenhower's "new look" defense policy argued that the U.S. missile program was defective, and that by the early 1960's, a "missile gap" would emerge to give the Soviet's nuclear superiority over America.

Richard Aliano (D−1) has examined the extensive debate about the missile gap from 1957 to 1961. The dispute developed because Eisenhower's "new look" defense policy had stabilized the defense budget after 1953. Whereas Truman's final defense program called for an escalation of defense expenditures from about $40 to $80 billion annually, Eisenhower's Administration placed a ceiling of between $40 and $45 billion on defense costs in an attempt to balance the federal budget. To achieve this goal, Eisenhower established priorities for defense needs. He emphasized America's nuclear weapons while slashing the budgets for conventional forces of the army and navy. Even the U.S. Air Force had to carefully allocate its expenditures to fit Eisenhower's programs.

American military interests did not appreciate Eisenhower's program. Even before the Soviet Union's successes of 1957, leaders of the military−industrial−academic complex organized opposition to the "new look" program and to Eisenhower's attempts to encourage Khrushchev's peaceful coexistence policy. Led by Republicans such as Nelson Rockefeller and Democrats such as Lyndon B. Johnson, the "new look" opponents used the news media and congressional hearings to criticize Eisenhower's program. The Sputnik launching of 1957 and Khrushchev's "rocket" boasts greatly aided these critics.

The "missile−gap" claim of Eisenhower's critics became the most effective of their arguments. Using estimates of the Soviet Union's missile production capacity, they conjectured that Khrushchev could deploy enough ICBM's by the early 1960's to successfully threaten America's heretofore unquestioned nuclear advantage. If the "missile gap" occurred, the U.S. could suffer political defeats in all parts of the world unless it was willing to risk the possibility of nuclear war.

President Eisenhower tried to convince the U.S. public that his critics were wrong. He appointed James Killian as a special science advisor to explain the technical reasons why there would be no "missile gap." As noted in their memoirs, both Killian and his successor, George Kistiakowsky, knew there was no missile gap but could not effectively answer all the hypothetical, frequently absurd, suppositions of Eisenhower's critics. The president agreed to increase the missile defense budget in 1958−59 but could not, from a budget−balancing standpoint, accept each of the large defense expenditures which such critics as Henry Kissinger and General Maxwell Taylor proposed.

While the president's critics projected a theoretical future missile-gap, Eisenhower's intelligence data convinced him there was no evidence of a missile gap developing by the early 1960's. Edgar M. Bottome (D-3) has an excellent discussion of why, in spite of Eisenhower being right, his critics were able to create the missile-gap myth of 1960. While critics used the number of missiles Moscow *could* deploy, Eisenhower relied on data which assessed the missiles they actually produced. Moreover, Eisenhower relied on America's diversified capability of manned bombers as well as ICBM's to deter the Soviets, while his critics stressed only the number of ICBM's the two sides might have. Secretary of Defense Neil McElroy told Congress in 1959 that Eisenhower did not intend to try and "match missile for missile in the ICBM category of Russian capability....Our position is that our diversified capability to deliver the big weapon [nuclear warheads] is what we are going to count as our ability to deter general war."[10]

Nevertheless, the President refused to disclose the secret data collected from U-2 spy plane flights and other CIA sources which would show that Moscow was not producing the large numbers of ICBM's Khushchev boasts implied. Without such data, Eisenhower could not quiet his critics who contended Ike was "weak" on security issues just as he had been on the "loss of Cuba." During the 1960 campaign, Kennedy was a proponent of the missile-gap thesis and condemned the Republicans for refusing to spend the money necessary to protect America.

Soon after his election, President Kennedy pushed quickly to enlarge the nation's conventional and nuclear defenses, even though Secretary of Defense Robert McNamara had realized as early as February 1961, that there was no missile gap. Although Roger Hilsman, who Kennedy appointed as Director of the State Department's Intelligence Bureau, claims conclusive evidence of the Soviet lag was not obtained until "the summer and fall" of 1961, Secretary McNamara told reporters on February 6, there was "no sign of a Soviet crash effort to build ICBMS...."[11]

For the Cuban missile crisis, the critical factor regarding the missile-gap issue was that late in 1961, Kennedy deflated Khrushchev's boasts of rocket parity and publicly emphasized that Russia's missile program lagged far behind that of the United States. On October 21, 1961, Deputy Secretary of Defense Roswell Gilpatric stated that the U.S. had "a second strike capability which is at least as extensive as what the Soviets can deliver by striking first." In short, the U.S.

continued to have strategic nuclear superiority. Gilpatric's speech was a deliberate decision to tell the Soviets that America knew the Soviets were deficient in nuclear−tipped ICBM's. In early November, both Kennedy and McNamara announced that U.S. military power was "second to none." McNamara asserted, "I believe we have nuclear power several times that of the Soviet Union."[12]

The American disclosure that the Soviet nuclear capacity was inferior was not news to Khrushchev. It was, however, a shock to the Soviet Union's allies in East Europe, China and the Third World who had believed Khrushchev's rocket boasts. Coming at the same time − November 1961 − that the Sino−Soviet dispute became public, Khrushchev was twice embarrassed.

The reason for the Soviet missile lag seems clear. Although the Soviet Union could have built more ICBM's after 1957 as Eisenhower's critics had contended, the Russian leaders decided in 1958 against the immediate construction and deployment of large numbers of ICBM's. There were at least three reasons why Moscow delayed its ICBM program. First, within the Soviet military regime, the Red Army commanded the largest following. Its priority was to devote the bulk of military expenditures to defense measures in Europe. Khrushchev could not easily overcome the Red Army's influence. Secondly, Khrushchev's post−Stalin program emphasized funds for Soviet consumer goods, domestic products which Stalin had strictly limited. Finally, the Soviet leaders chose to do what Eisenhower had done; that is, to withhold deployment of first generation liquid−fuel missiles in order to save funds for the second generation solid−fuel rockets. Most, but not all, rocket experts believed the liquid−fuel missiles were too dangerous and too slow to launch under crisis circumstances. Solid−fuel weapons could be based with immediate launching readiness and, sooner or later, would be the missile to be reckoned with. For the Russian rocket program, this meant delaying their ICBM program until 1964. Eisenhower had also given most of his funds to the solid−fuel program and by 1960−61, Kennedy's missile build−up reaped the rewards of Ike's wisdom. America's solid−fuel missiles were technically ahead of the Soviet Union's.[13]

The Kennedy administration's disclosure of Khrushchev's deceptive boasts about Russian rockets, plus its acceleration of America's missile program became costly blows to Soviet power and prestige. Consequently in 1962, Khrushchev sought to reduce America's nuclear superiority. Without nuclear parity with the U.S., Khrushchev's desire for nuclear free zones in Europe and Asia would be stalled by Washington. In this context, what was now the Soviet's missile gap could be partly closed by establishing IRBM and MRBM missile bases in Cuba capable of hitting many Western Hemispheric cities. From a strategic missile standpoint, this was a principle reason why the U.S.S.R. placed missiles in Cuba.

In order to enhance the Soviet's strategic position by sending IRBM's and MRBM's to Cuba, Khrushchev had to manipulate the Soviet bureaucracy. As described by Michael Tatu (P−14) and Roman Kolkowicz (P−10), Khrushchev replaced the head of Russia's Strategic Rocket forces, Marshal K. S. Moskalenko, with one of his Ukrainian clients, S. S. Biryuzov. Moskalenko, an artillery−trained officer, represented the older Red Army class which wanted the rockets to support the ground forces in defending the U.S.S.R. from a European invasion. Biryuzov backed the concepts of Khrushchev and other younger Soviet rocket officers who proposed a strategic role for nuclear weapons and arrangements to off−set America's ICBM superiority. Consequently, Biryuzov supported Khrushchev in the placing of missiles in Cuba as an expedient to deny America a first−strike option against the Soviet Union.[14]

Thus, Khrushchev's decision to base missiles in Cuba was, in part, a means of improving the Soviet's strategic nuclear position. If Cuban bases were established, the Soviet leaders could hope to neutralize America's nuclear superiority, employ diplomacy to obtain nuclear free zones in Central Europe and China, and resolve favorably the issue of Berlin and a divided Germany.

KHRUSHCHEV AND CASTRO

The Soviet decision to construct a missile base in Cuba was also related to Khrushchev's desire to lead the Third World revolutions. During the early 1960's, Fidel Castro appeared as the principal symbol of nationalistic attempts to end their colonial relationships with Western nations. Although fourth in order of Soviet priorities relative to the missile crisis, aid to Castro served the Soviets well as an irritant to Washington. As wars of national liberation arose in colonial regions after 1945, communist sponsorship of the rebels had resulted in at least two changes in American foreign policy. First, it led the U.S. to end its traditional opposition to colonialism and to begin supporting counter—revolutionary forces. Secondly, it led the U.S. to expend money and incur casualties by engaging in counterinsurgency programs.

During World War II, President Franklin D. Roosevelt urged France and Great Britain to give up their colonial holdings. Initially, President Truman retained this policy but gradually, as the Cold War began, Truman's containment policy expanded from U.S. efforts to defend Europe against Soviet encroachments to a global effort which would maintain wherever possible the status quo in the "free world." During the 1950's, colonial wars of liberation succeeded despite American opposition. The British, French, Dutch, Portuguese and Belgians all lost most of their imperial possessions. The British usually sought non—military solutions which permitted its withdrawal from colonies while retaining some economic and political influence. The French, Dutch, and Portuguese engaged in costly wars in South and Southeast Asia, and in Africa. Subsequently, when during its September 1960 session, the United Nations admitted 16 new nations, the Afro—Asian group became the largest voting bloc in the General Assembly.

The United States had not, however, found a suitable technique for dealing with wars of national liberation. The CIA intervened in Iran in 1953 to assist in overthrowing the nationalist leader, Mohamed Mossadeg, and in restoring the Shah to power. Similarly, in Central America, the U.S. acted in 1954 to support the overthrow of a left—wing Guatamalan government and restore a friendly military regime. However, from 1955 to 1960, Eisenhower generally opposed intervention in national liberation conflicts. Critics such as General Taylor and Senator John F. Kennedy argued that Eisenhower's reduction of funds for the army prevented the creation of suitable counterinsurgency forces.[15]

Kennedy's criticism of Eisenhower was dramatized during the 1960 U.N. session because no figures became more prominent media "friends" than Fidel Castro and Nikita Khrushchev. Laughing and embracing each other for newsphotos and television shots, the Cuban—Soviet comrades seemed to depict Soviet gains in the Third World at the expense of the United States. They also sought to persuade China that Moscow was the proper leader of Third World movements. Thus by embracing Castro in 1960, Khrushchev allied the Soviet Union with a forthright spokesman for liberation. Castro also gained. He obtained a friend to protect him from the United States as well as from professional communists in Cuba who desired to overthrow him.

In 1962, Cuba became a logical location for Khrushchev to undertake his gamble for an impressive foreign policy victory over the United States. Cuba was a liberated Third World power which desired Moscow's protection. Moreover, it was far enough away from the Russian homeland to make it a low-risk Soviet venture, but close enough to America to enable Soviet intermediate range missiles to be as effective as ICBMs. Operated by Soviet army personnel, the Soviet missile bases in Cuba could promote the Kremlin's international political goals in Central Europe and Asia, equalize Soviet and U.S. strategic powers, and dramatize Moscow's intention to aid national liberation.[16]

KHRUSHCHEV'S ESCALATION OF AID TO CUBA, 1960–1962

Even before the Presidium's 1962 decision to base missiles in Cuba, Khrushchev had escalated his assistance to Castro between 1960 and July 1962. Herbert Dinerstein (P-3) has documented the exchanges between Moscow and Havana which enunciated the growing cooperation between Castro and Khrushchev.

The Soviet leader first suggested that Cuba could be protected by the Soviet nuclear umbrella as early as July 9, 1960. Shortly after Washington cut-off Cuba's sugar quota in June 1960, Khrushchev told a Soviet teacher's convention in a televised speech that Cuba was in danger because the U.S. planned to strangle the Cuban economy as a prelude to military invasion. If the U.S. should attack Cuba, he said, the U.S.S.R. would protect them because "Soviet artillerymen can support the Cuban people with their rocket fire." The Soviet Union had rockets which "can land precisely on targets 13,000 kilometers away." Thus, the Chairman concluded, this is "...a warning to those who would like to solve international problems by force and not reason."[17] Khrushchev had rattled Soviet rockets before. This was the first time, however, he extended the rockets to the protection of Cuba. Both Castro and the Cuban Foreign Minister Raul Rao welcomed Soviet ICBM rockets as a deterrent to further U.S. threats.

Three days later, July 12, Khrushchev made another statement which pleased Cubans but antagonized Americans. He told a Moscow news conference that "the Monroe Doctrine has outlived its time." It has "died a natural death." This doctrine, he said, had allowed the United States to perpetuate its control over Latin America, and it was no longer valid. The Soviets sympathized with the just demands of all colonial people and would aid them against their U.S. oppressors.

The April 1961 Bay of Pigs incident resulted in further Khrushchev rhetoric. On April 15, he notified Kennedy that the Soviets were ready to aid Cuba, warning that direct U.S. intervention in Cuba could "lead the world to military catastrophe." Although Kennedy had previously decided not to commit any U.S. forces to salvage the landing attempt, both the Russians and Cubans believed Khrushchev's warning had persuaded Kennedy to cancel the second bomber attack on April 17, a decision which helped defeat the invasion effort.

In the aftermath of the Bay of Pigs, the Cuban leaders were convinced that the U.S. would again try to invade their island. Castro urged Moscow to not only augment Cuba's conventional forces but to also make explicit Khrushchev's statement that he would use ICBM's if necessary to deter or defeat any American attack. The Soviet leaders hesitated to define precisely how they would use Soviet-based missiles in the event the U.S. attacked Cuba. While it was a good tactic not to be explicit, Khrushchev realized that the Soviet's intercontinental capability was not sufficient to help Cuba. Therefore, Kennedy's November 1961 announcement of the U.S. ICBM superiority and the Soviet weaknesses shook Cuba's confidence.[18]

Throughout the period from April 1961 to October 1962, Kennedy continually declared the U.S. would not abandon Cuba to communism. On April 20, the president told a meeting of news editors: "I want it clearly understood that this government will not hesitate in meeting its primary obligations" to ensure the nation's security. If necessary, he stated, the U.S. would not fail to intervene in Cuba simply because it was "lectured on intervention by those whose character was stamped for all time in the bloody streets of Budapest."[19] If Russia could send troops to Hungary in 1956, the president implied, the U.S. could send them to Cuba if it was found essential.

During early 1962, attacks on Cuba by exiles from Miami and New York haunted Cuba while the U.S. urged the Organization of America States (OAS) to isolate Cubans from the other Western Hemispheric states as long as the communists remained in power. Thus, in the context of Cuba's dangers and the Soviet's global interests, Khrushchev and the Soviet Union's Presidium agreed sometime between January and July 1962, to secretly construct the missile bases that would be operational in Cuba by mid-November. Michael Tatu contends the Presidium's decision was made in late April; however, Herbert

Dinerstein believes the first Soviet statement formulating a suitable rationale for placing missiles in Cuba, was issued on February 18, 1962. The February statement by the Soviet government on the Cuban problem appealed to "all peace—loving" peoples to back Cuba against America's aggression. The U.S., the Soviet article said, must learn to coexist with neighbors of different political systems just as the U.S.S.R. coexists with Finland and other neighbors who have American missile bases. If the U.S. could restrict its Western Hemispheric neighbors while it also extended missile bases to the Soviet borders, the Kremlin would reassess its policy and, like America, restrict its European neighbors and protect countries friendly to Russia in all parts of the world.

As Dinerstein notes, the February 18 article laid the general basis for justifying a Soviet missile base in the Western hemisphere. On July 27, Fidel Castro delivered a speech which contained a more clear indication that the Soviet Union would provide Cuba with effective defense assistance. Speaking optimistically about Cuba's future, Castro asserted that the U.S. must realize that its attempt to isolate Cuba had failed. The Soviet Union had sent Havana sufficient arms to eliminate the fear of an invasion by mercenaries; now, Cuba needed only to be able to repel a direct American attack. To achieve this, Castro asserted, Cuba was taking measures which would make any such invasion a World War. These defense measures would either deter or shatter "a direct imperialist attack." The Soviet Union and other socialist nations, he said, have joined Cuba in making a great investment to jointly resist the dangers of further imperialist attacks.[20]

Although Castro's July statement did not precisely say Soviet missiles were on their way to Cuba, in retrospect his message seems to indicate significant changes in Cuba—Soviet defense policies that would greatly improve upon the conventional arms Moscow had already supplied. Within one month, on August 29, 1962, the United States obtained concrete evidence that Soviet surface—to—air (SAM) missile sites were being constructed in Cuba.

In brief, the Soviet decision to place missiles in Cuba was not impulsive. If as the Soviet leaders expected, they could construct missile bases before the U.S. acted, the Soviet "missile—gap" would end. A low—risk effort could bring great rewards. Cuba would be protected, enhancing Soviet prestige in the Third World; Moscow could press Washington to accept its terms on Berlin and Germany; nuclear free zones could be gained in Central Europe and Asia to increase Soviet security; and America would have to recognize Soviet equality in the international political—military community. Khrushchev's gamble in Cuba appeared to hold the promise of excellent rewards at minimum expense to the Soviets in either rubles or risks.

Khrushchev and the Presidium acted secretly in Cuba to prevent the U.S. from reacting effectively until the bases were operational. If the gamble worked, Khrushchev would attend the United Nations in mid—November 1962 and announce that he had given Cuba a "defense" force. His coup would gain Third World support as well as aid from socialist nations. Together they would stop U.S. efforts to remove the Cuban missiles. The U.S.S.R. would achieve a step forward in obtaining nuclear parity with America.

NOTES

1. John F. Kennedy, *Public Papers of the Presidents: John F. Kennedy — 1962* (Washington, DC: G.P.O., 1963), 806–808.

2. Schlesinger, *Thousand Days*, 796, 821.

3. Roger Hilsman and Ronald Steel, "An Exchange of Views," *New York Review of Books* 12 (May 8, 1969), 17–21; Ronald Steel, "Endgame, Thirteen Days," *New York Review of Books* 12 (Mar. 13, 1969), 15–22; Major General Max Johnson (ret.), "Who Really Gained in the Cuban Showdown?" *U.S. News and World Report* 53 (Nov. 12, 1962), 45. In his memoir, Robert Kennedy says Air Force Chief of Staff General Curtis LeMay wanted to attack Cuba on October 28 even after Khrushchev had yielded, *Thirteen Days* (New York: Norton, 1969), 119.

4. Transcript of Recording of ExCom Sessions on October 16, 1962, *John F. Kennedy Library*, especially read session 1 which began at 11:45 a.m. Hereafter cited as *ExCom Sess. Oct. 16*.

5. On the "testing of will" issue see Graham Allison, *Essence of Decision* (Boston: Little, Brown, 1971), 50–52. Arthur Schlesinger does not

emphasize the "will" idea in *Robert F. Kennedy and His Times* (Boston: Houghton Mifflin, 1978), 525–531, 554. Perhaps, Sorensen first brought up this idea in a memo of October 17, see Barton Bernstein, "The Week We Almost Went to War," *Bulletin of the Atomic Scientists* 32 (Feb. 1976), 16, fn. 27. The idea may have been appealing to Sorensen and Schlesinger in 1962 because scholars of deterrence used the analogy of the "chicken" game at that time. See Robert Jervis, "Deterrence Theory Revisited," *World Politics* 31 (Jan. 1979), 289–292. This is no minor issue because "credibility" and "will" influenced both Kennedy and Johnson from 1962 to 1969. See Richard N. LeBow, "The Cuban Missile Crisis: Reading the Lessons Correctly," *Political Science Quarterly* 98 (Fall 1983), 431–455.

6. Stephen S. Kaplan, *Diplomacy of Power: Soviet Armed Forces as a Political Instrument*, (Washington, DC: Brookings Institution, 1981), especially pages 1–60; John H. Hodgson, "Soviet Foreign Policy: Mental Alienation on Universal Revolution," *Western Political Quarterly* 24 (Dec. 1971), 653–665.

7. Adam Ulam, *Expansion and Coexistence: The History of Soviet Foreign Policy* (New York: Praeger, 1968), 284–301; Michael Tatu, *Power in the Kremlin: From Khrushchev to Kosygin*, translated by Helen Katel (New York: Viking, 1969), 232–233; Jack M. Schick, *The Berlin Crisis 1958–1962* (Philadelphia: University of Pennsylvania Press, 1971), 138–141 and 207–212.

8. Edward Crankshaw, *The New Cold War: Moscow vs. Peking* (Baltimore: Penguin, 1963), 20–96; Ulam, *Expansion and Coexistence*, 301–325, Robert Crane, "The Cuban Crisis: A Strategic Analysis of American and Soviet Policy," *Orbis* 6 (Winter 1963), 528–563.

9. Crankshaw, "New Cold War", 97–135.

10. Richard Aliano, *American Defense Policy from Eisenhower to Kennedy* (Athens: Ohio University Press, 1975), 70–99; Edgar Bottome, *The Balance of Terror* (Boston: Beacon, 1971), 39–73.

11. Desmond Ball, *Politics and Force Levels* (Berkeley: University of California Press, 1980), 3–104; Roger Hilsman, *To Move A Nation* (New York: Delta, 1967), 162–163; McNamara as quoted in the

Washington Post, Feb. 7, 1961. After news headlines stated there was no missile gap, President Kennedy's press secretary said the statements were "absolutely wrong and studies on the issue had not been completed." For analysis of the timing, see Ball, *Politics and Force Levels*, 89–99.

12. Hilsman, *To Move A Nation*, 163–164; Ball, *Politics and Force Levels*, 98–99.

13. Tatu, *Power in the Kremlin*, 236–7; Roman Kolkowicz, *Conflicts in Soviet Party–Military Relations 1962–1963* (Santa Monica, CA: Rand Corp., 1963), 5–11.

14. Tatu, *Power in the Kremlin*, 230–239.

15. Richard A. Falk, "Counterrevolution in the Modern World: Soviet–American Consensus and Continuities Between Counterinsurgency Abroad and at Home," in Lynn H. Miller and Ronald W. Pruessen, eds. *Reflections on the Cold War* (Philadelphia: Temple University Press, 1974), 183–201; Richard Barnet, *Intervention and Revolution* (New York: New American Library, 1968), 62–115.

16. Ulam, *Expansion and Coexistence*, 313–314; Facts on File, *Cuba, The U.S. and Russia*, 18–20; on the low–risk estimate see Alexander George and Richard Smoke, *Deterrence in American Foreign Policy* (New York: Columbia University Press, 1974), 461–465. On the risk issue George Ball informed the ExCom on October 16, that Roger Hilsman's "demonologists" in the State Department believed the situation was low–risk, but Ambassador Thompson thought it was high–risk for Russia. *ExCom Sess. Oct. 16*, second session, 40–41.

17. Dinerstein, *Making A Missile Crisis*, 80–83.

18. *Ibid.*, 83–111.

19. J. F. Kennedy, *Public Papers–1961*, 304–306.

20. Tatu, *Power in the Kremlin*, 230–235; Dinerstein, *Making a Missile Crisis*, 166–168.

III

U.S. Detects Soviet Missiles in Cuba

On August 29, 1962, the Kennedy Administration obtained its first definitive evidence that Soviet surface−to−air missiles (SAMs) were being based in Cuba. Surveillance flights by U−2 planes photographed Soviet technicians constructing SAM launching pads. The SAM was a defensive weapon used to shoot down invading aircraft. In 1960, for example, a SAM shot down Gary Powers' U−2 which was flying a photographic mission over Soviet territory.

DOMESTIC POLITICS AND THE CUBAN CRISIS

The American public learned about the Soviet missile activity in Cuba from one of Kennedy's Republican critics, Senator Kenneth Keating of New York. In a manner which Keating never disclosed, CIA data on the Cuban−based SAMs was leaked to the Senator who used the information to launch Republican congressional attacks on the Kennedy Administration. The August U−2 data on Soviet surface−to−air missiles especially fit the Republican Congressional Committee's decision to focus the fall congressional elections on claims that Kennedy had been "weak" in combating Cuban communism since becoming president. On August 31, Keating told the Senate that there was evidence of Soviet "rocket installations in Cuba." He urged Kennedy to act vigorously, proposing that the Organization of American States (OAS) send an investigating team to Cuba.[1]

Keating's speech inaugurated an intensive political dispute about United States−Cuban policy, a dispute which the *New York Times* termed a crisis during September 1962. Republicans such as Senators Barry Goldwater and Homer Capehart joined in lambasting Kennedy's failure to counteract the Soviet military build−up in Cuba. On August

34 The Missile Crisis

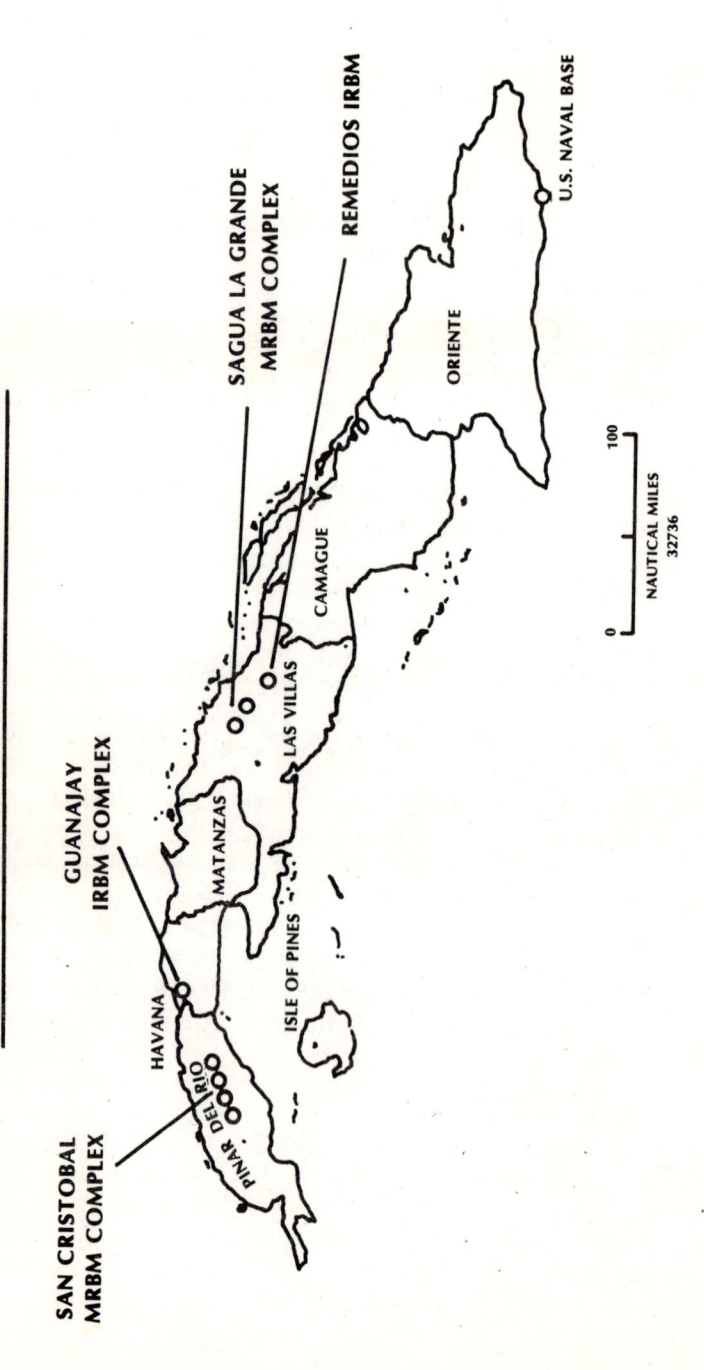

LOCATION OF MRBM AND IRBM SITES IN CUBA

28, Capehart claimed there were Soviet combat troops in Cuba. On September 2, Senator Strom Thurmond urged that the U.S. invade Cuba and destroy Castro's regime.

A variety of factors fueled the September crisis. On August 25, a Cuban exile group shelled Miramar, a Havana suburb, with 20mm cannons fired from motor launches off–shore. Cuban exile groups such as Alpha 66 staged anti–Castro demonstrations and announced plans to attack Cuba. On August 28, Moscow announced it was doubling the materials it was sending to Cuba, chartering West European ships to carry the supplies. The Kennedy Administration failed to persuade its NATO allies, such as Great Britain, to stop using their ships to carry supplies to Cuba. The British refusal prompted the House of Representatives to propose cutting off economic aid to nations engaged in Cuban trade.

Republicans took more direct action to put Kennedy on the spot. On September 7, Senator Everett Dirksen and Representative Charles Halleck introduced a Joint Congressional Resolution which authorized the president to use U.S. troops against Cuba. Before the proposal passed Congress, the Democrats successfully watered down the resolution and its effect. When signed on October 4, the resolution sanctioned the use of U.S. forces, if necessary, to defend the Western Hemisphere from aggression or subversion by Cuba. It also pledged America to work with the OAS and "freedom–loving Cubans" to obtain self–determination.[2]

Because of these Republican ploys, the Kennedy Administration tended to treat the CIA data on the SAMs in the context of domestic politics rather than fully exploring the missiles' military and foreign policy implications. Although Kennedy consulted with CIA Director John McCone when the SAMs were first located, he did not do so following the political attacks by Keating and Capehart at the end of August because McCone was honeymooning in Europe.

Before issuing his statements of September 4 and 13 on the evidence of Soviet activity in Cuba, Kennedy consulted principally with his two advisors on domestic affairs, Robert Kennedy and Theodore Sorensen. The president's subsequent statements were therefore to reassure the American public as much as to warn the Soviet Union. The thrust of his statements was that there was no evidence of Soviet weapons other than those adding to Cuba's defense; however, if evidence of Soviet offensive missiles were discovered the president would do whatever was necessary to protect U.S. security.

The key paragraph of the September 4 statement read:

> There is no evidence of any organized combat forces in Cuba from any Soviet bloc country; of military bases provided to Russia; of a violation of the 1934 treaty relating to Guantanamo; of the presence of offensive ground-to-ground missiles; or of other significant offensive capability either in Cuban hands or under Soviet direction and guidance. Were it to be otherwise, the gravest issues would arise.

Similarly, the central part of the September 13 message was that if Cuba should "become an offensive base of significant capacity for the Soviet Union, then this country will do whatever must be done to protect its own security and that of its allies."

Although the president, his brother and Sorensen believed they issued a strong warning, neither statement matched the other instances of vigorous exchanges and stern rhetoric between Moscow and Washington since 1945. Much of Kennedy's warning hinged on the definition of "offensive" and "defensive" weapons. During the September 13 conference, a reporter asked Kennedy to clarify the meaning of "offensive" but the president did not do so.[3] More importantly, the general tone of Kennedy's statements were moderate because he sought to reassure Americans as well as to warn Khrushchev. Kennedy wanted to counteract the domestic impact of the charges of Keating, Capehart, Thurmond, and others by showing firmness. At the same time, however, he did not want to raise tensions with Moscow by seeming abrasive.

Kennedy also used private contacts with the Soviet Union in an effort to lessen tensions with the Kremlin. Robert Kennedy spoke with Soviet Ambassador Anatoly F. Dobrynin on September 4, while Theodore Sorensen spoke with him two days later. Judging by the memoirs of Kennedy (M−34) and Sorensen (M−7) both told the ambassador of America's concern for the Soviet activity in Cuba. Dobrynin assured them that the Soviet aid to Castro was only for defensive purposes. He told Robert Kennedy that the Soviets would not put ground-to-ground missiles in Cuba. In addition, Dobrynin commented that Khrushchev wanted President Kennedy to know the Soviets would refrain from any aggressive activity prior to the November elections. Although this comment puzzled the president's advisors, they did not explore this unusual statement with American experts on Soviet behavior. Neither Sorensen nor the president's brother appeared to have spoken forcefully or with particular alarm regarding the missiles because they believed the Republican warnings were motivated by politics, not hard facts.[4]

Deterrence policy requires the early perception, communication, and cessation of either super power's nuclear challenge. As Alexander George and Richard Smoke (R−4) explain, Kennedy's September warnings did not meet these requirements. The September statements were so mild that they misled the Soviet calculations of American attitudes toward the Cuban missile construction. At the same time, they were considered sufficiently binding to prompt Kennedy and his advisors to react strongly when definite evidence of the Soviet's medium range missiles in Cuba was discovered in October. Thus, the October crisis became dangerous because of the Republican political criticism, Kennedy's relatively mild warnings, and the Soviet deception in their September responses. The combination of these factors placed Kennedy on the defensive by October because he promised to do whatever was necessary to eliminate any "offensive" Soviet capabilities found in Cuba.

Equally critical, however, was that once Khrushchev committed Soviet missiles to Castro, it was difficult for the Kremlin to reverse itself. As McGeorge Bundy, Kennedy's National Security Advisor noted on October 16, after the Soviet medium range missiles were discovered, Khrushchev had obviously made his decision on the missile project in June. Once the gamble had begun, the President's September statements were too late to dissuade Khrushchev. As the President acknowledged to Bundy: "I guess I needed to make an explicit warning earlier this summer."[5]

In retrospect, the Kennedy−Bundy exchange appears correct. The Soviet arms build−up in Cuba had increased significantly during the year following the Bay of Pigs. Yet as these conventional arms shipments escalated, no U.S. statements warned Khrushchev of the limits of U.S. forbearance or at what point these shipments might become unacceptable. Although Roger Hilsman believes that U.S. intelligence had been concerned earlier about possible missiles in Cuba, records available thus far do not indicate any clear American suspicion, prior to August 1962, that nuclear missiles might be based in Cuba.[6]

DELAY IN THE DISCOVERY OF OFFENSIVE WEAPONS

President Kennedy's desire in September to assure the American public that the Republican charges were exaggerated also influenced important high level decisions of two national security committees. First, on September 10, Secretary of State Rusk persuaded the Committee on Overhead Reconnaissance (COMOR) to stop all U−2 flights over Cuban territory where the SAMs had been sighted. The day before COMOR met, the Chinese Communists had shot down a U−2 plane being "loaned" to the National Chinese on Formosa. Recalling the damage done to Eisenhower's political position when the Russians downed an American U−2 in May 1960, Rusk convinced COMOR that such an incident should be avoided.

Consequently from September 10 to October 14, no U−2 flights took place over the precise areas where the Soviets were constructing the MRBM and IRBM sites. Only after CIA Director McCone returned from a four-week honeymoon and urged the resumption of flights over western Cuba did the COMOR cancel this prohibition. The U−2 flight of October 14 discovered the Soviet missile construction. Although Roger Hilsman contends little time was lost by the delayed U−2 information, he admits the sites might have been discovered by a "stroke of luck" on or after September 21. The main point is, however, that the COMOR decision restricting U−2 flights resulted largely from domestic political considerations. Keating's partisan attacks had aggravated the problem and Kennedy's political instincts had caused him to react defensively.

Kennedy's September statements also influenced decisions of the U.S. Intelligence Board (USIB). After its September 19 meeting, the USIB issued a National Intelligence Estimate (NIE) which stated the Soviet Union did *not* intend to place offensive missiles in Cuba. As Hilsman asserts, although the NIE underscored the advantages which Russia could gain from a Cuban missile base and "urged the intelligence community to maintain a continuous alert," the NIE calculated that the risk was too high for Khrushchev to attempt to base offensive missiles in Cuba.

In addition to the domestic political influences on the USIB, analysts find two other errors contributing to the NIE's miscalculation of Soviet intentions. First, as Alexander George and Richard Smoke have pointed out, the USIB erred because it incorrectly assessed the Soviet's risk calculation. The USIB thought the Soviet Union was too cautious in the control of its nuclear missiles to send them to Cuba. Since Moscow had never stationed missiles in Warsaw Pact nations, the USIB believed the Soviets would consider Castro too unstable to be trusted with them. The NIE concluded, therefore, that its "best guess" of Soviet intentions was that there were no plans for offensive missiles in Cuba. This "best guess" corresponded with President Kennedy's September position that the public could be assured that Soviet offensive missiles would not be sent to Cuba.[7]

Finally, as Arthur Krock (E-7), Elie Abel (A-1) and Graham Allison indicate, U.S. intelligence operation had been affected by John McCone's absence. McCone was honeymooning on the French Riviera throughout September. Just before leaving Washington in late August, McCone had been the only person in the administration who warned Kennedy that Moscow might decide to base offensive missiles in Cuba. In meeting with the president on August 22, a week before the U-2 photos disclosed the SAMs, McCone conjectured that Khrushchev might gamble on missile bases in Cuba. Later, on August 29, McCone was the only Kennedy official who believed Khrushchev's plans went beyond the SAM bases. On both these occasions, McCone's reputation as an ardent anti-communist prevented serious consideration of his opinions. Because others saw McCone as a devil's advocate in all discussions, his warnings on Soviet intentions were routinely downgraded by his colleagues and the president.

McCone's September honeymoon meant that no one on COMOR or USIB, argued the view for Soviet duplicity. In September, McCone sent five telegrams concerning Russian missile deployment to his CIA deputy, General Marshall Carter, but Carter did not distribute these messages outside the CIA. Carter thought McCone had presented his views to Kennedy and other officials before leaving town.[8]

During September, therefore, President Kennedy adopted — and COMOR and USIB followed — a prescription designed to calm the U.S. public by assuming the Soviets would not undertake the risk of placing offensive missiles in Cuba. Although Kennedy's policy of reassuring the American public led him on September 7 to ask Congressional authority to call up 15,000 reserves, the strongest legislative move on the Cuban situation came from Republicans seeking to harass Kennedy. The Republicans introduced a congressional resolution condemning Castro's activity in Latin America, which passed September 26, because Democrats could not afford to vote against it. As worded, the resolution condemned Castro's effort to export revolution and to build up Cuba's conventional weapons. Its language, however, was more bellicose than Kennedy's, stating that the U.S. should "prevent by whatever means necessary, including the use of arms, the Marxist—Leninist regime in Cuba extending by force or the threat of force, its aggressive activities to any part of the hemisphere." In Moscow, this resolution may or may not have been taken as part of America's domestic politics. Its only apparent significance was to make Kennedy vulnerable to future Republican attacks once Soviet offensive missiles were discovered in Cuba.9

During early October, the prevailing lassitude of the Kennedy Administration caused a further delay in sending U-2 flights over the areas of western Cuba where the SAM missiles had been spotted. After returning from the Riveria, McCone met with COMOR on October 4, urging them to risk a U-2 flight over the SAM base area of Cuba; however, McCone's proposal and COMOR's postive response was not acted on for another ten days.

After COMOR scheduled a U-2 flight over western Cuba where the SAMs were being constructed, a bureaucratic squabble resulted. Although the allegation is denied in the official Senate Armed Service Committee Report (E-11), Abel and Allison both believe representatives of the Air Force's Strategic Air Command and the CIA argued over who should pilot the U-2 flights over Cuba. The Air Force insisted that uniformed officers should do so. The CIA countered that it flew improved, modified U-2s which required special training to operate. The State Department entered the fray, urging COMOR to reconsider the high-risks involved. Eventually the Air Force won the dispute. Whether or not an Air Force flight failed on October 9 is unconfirmed. On October 14, however, following training by the CIA, Air Force Major Rudolf Anderson, Jr., flew over western Cuba.10

Anderson's photos revealed that launching pads were being constructed for Soviet MRBM and IRBM ground-to-ground missiles in Cuba. Although on October 14, Anderson's photos did not locate any nuclear warhead storage facilities, these missiles were designed to carry such warheads. During the next two weeks, U-2 photos and other intelligence operations identified a wide variety of Soviet military equipment in Cuba. Together with the missile bases under construction, this equipment included:

1. *MRBMs.* There were six sites, each having four launch positions capable of firing two missiles each. This totaled 48 MRBMs with an effective range of 1,020 nautical

miles. In its October 28 report, the CIA stated all MRBM launchers were in operation. The CIA located nuclear storage facilities but found no nuclear warheads.

2. *IRBMs*. There were 3 fixed sites under construction, each having four launch positions. This totaled twelve launchers with a range of 2,200 nautical miles. On October 25, the CIA estimated one base would be operational by December 1, the other two by December 15. No IRBM warheads reached Cuba.

3. *IL−28 Bombers*. Forty−two unassembled IL−28 (Beagle) bombers arrived at two Cuban airfields in early October. Only seven of these planes were finally assembled. The bombers had a round−trip range of 600 nautical miles.

4. *SAMs*. Twenty−four SAM−2 sites formed a tight perimeter air defense for the MRBM and IRBM sites. Each SAM site had six launchers with missiles in place and three reload missiles available. These anti−aircraft weapons could hit targets at 80,000 feet altitude and had a horizontal range of 30 nautical miles. Most SAMs became operational by October 23.

5. *Cruise Naval Missiles*. There were four Soviet coastal cruise missile sites in Cuba. They were located near key beaches and harbors. Each site had 34−foot launchers, guidance equipment and a number of conventionally armed missiles with a 40 nautical mile range. They were designed to defend against invading ships or amphibious operations.

6. *Guided Missile Patrol Boats*. The ports of Mariel and Banes held 12 high speed KOMAR patrol boats. Each carried two 20−foot cruise−type missiles with a range of 10 to 15 nautical miles.

7. *MIG−21 Aircraft*. Forty−two of the latest Soviet MIG−21 planes were in Cuba. They were designed to intercept aircraft with speeds of up to 1,000 knots at 40,000 feet, and carried air−to−air missiles. In addition, Cuba had received 40 MIG−15s and MIG−17s before July 1962.

8. *Soviet Armed Forces*. By October 22,000 Soviet soldiers and technicians were in Cuba to assemble, operate and defend Soviet weapons. Soviet infantry was at the four major missile installations, including a regimental−sized

armoured group equipped with 35 to 40 T−54 medium tanks, FROG tactical nuclear rockets with a 20−25 nautical mile range, and modern anti−tank missiles nicknamed the SNAPPER.[11]

Although the Soviet construction crews built the missile sites with remarkable speed, the delivery of the missiles and their operational status was handicapped by Soviet bureaucratic procedures. During the exporting and shipping of the missile equipment, the KGB utilized all the secret devices available to hide the materials. Once the ships reached Cuba, however, secrecy vanished. There was no camouflage at the missile sites until October 23, the day after Kennedy's disclosure of the U.S. discovery. Nor were the Soviet technical personnel hidden or made inconspicuous in Cuba. The SAMs should have been operational before construction began at the MRBM and IRBM sites, but they were not. Soviet radar which, unlike Cuban radar, could detect high−flying U−2 planes should have been operational early, but it was not.

Finally, the U.S. photos of the Soviet missile sites would have been more difficult to interpret if the Soviet engineers had varied their pattern of construction from that used in their homeland. For example, the Soviets built the exact unit insignia in their Cuban billeting area that was used in the Soviet Union. Each of these Soviet errors can be explained by Allison's organizational model as standard operating procedures. The Soviet agencies did not develop secret procedures to construct the Cuban bases. Each agency functioned as though it were on Soviet territory because they had never before built missile bases on foreign soil.

Despite these Soviet shortcomings, after October 14, American U−2 photographs of the Soviet's IRBM and MRBM construction sites indicated that Khrushchev had expanded his challenge to the U.S. in the Western Hemisphere. These missiles could hit a wide variety of American and Latin American targets, striking them in ten minutes or less as opposed to thirty minutes from the Soviet territory. Thus, the Kennedy Administration considered them to be offensive in nature and began to search for an appropriate response.[12]

JFK'S SEARCH FOR APPROPRIATE RESPONSE, OCT. 16-21

At 8:45 a.m. on Tuesday, October 16, William P. Bundy informed President Kennedy that U-2 photos taken two days earlier disclosed Soviet medium range missile sites under construction in Cuba. Immediately, the president called an 11:45 a.m. meeting of his high-level advisors, a group which became known as ExCom, the Executive Committee of the National Security Council.

The ExCom played a critical role in recommending action to President Kennedy between October 16 and October 29, 1962. Its members were Attorney General Robert Kennedy, Secretary of State Dean Rusk, Secretary of Defense Robert McNamara, Deputy Secretary of Defense Roswell Gilpatric, Assistant Secretary of Defense Paul Nitze, Chairman of the Joint Chiefs of Staff General Maxwell Taylor, CIA Director John McCone or his Deputy Director Marshall Carter, Secretary of the Treasury Douglas Dillon, White House Aides McGeorge Bundy and Theodore Sorensen, Undersecretary of State George Ball, Deputy Undersecretary of State Alexis Johnson, former Ambassador to the Soviet Union, Llewellyn Thompson, and Edwin Martin of the State Department's Latin American desk. At times, advisors such as Adlai Stevenson, Charles Bohlen and Dean Acheson met with the ExCom.[13]

In October 1983, the Kennedy Library released transcripts of the two ExCom sessions on October 16, 1962. While disclosing no sensational data, the transcripts did demonstrate the informal, free-wheeling exchange of ideas which took place in the ExCom sessions. The October 16 transcripts indicate that by the end of the day's two sessions, the ExCom had touched on each possible policy option that it would examine before recommending a naval blockade to the president on October 20.

During its first session which convened at 11:45 a.m., on October 16, the ExCom appeared to favor a U.S. air strike to remove the Soviet missile bases in Cuba. After first hearing Secretary of State Rusk's proposals for a diplomatic response, the ExCom members listened as Secretary of Defense McNamara outlined procedures for an air attack on Cuba. For the remainder of the noontime session and most of the evening session, the principal options discussed by the ExCom were (1) a single, quick surgical strike on the missile bases, (2) a broad air bombardment of various Cuban facilities, or (3) either of these two strikes plus a mopping-up invasion of Cuba. The air attacks would be surprise strikes and, as Secretary McNamara argued, they must be completed before the Soviet missiles were operational. The naval blockade, the proposal eventually recommended by the ExCom, was not suggested until about 7:30 p.m., near the end of the ExCom's evening session.

In order to clarify the ExCom's decision process, three aspects of their meetings between October 16 and 20 shall be reviewed: 1) the ExCom's analysis of possible Soviet motives; 2) its exploration of political—diplomatic options; and 3) its dicussion of military options, including its recommendation for a naval blockade.

Soviet Motives Assessed

Judging by the transcripts of the October 16 sessions, the ExCom members believed the Soviets had two likely motives: either Khrushchev desired to enhance Soviet strategic strength or he wished to trade the Cuban bases for Soviet advantages in Berlin or for removal of U.S. missile bases in Turkey or elsewhere. There was disagreement regarding the enhancement of Soviet strength. General Taylor believed the Cuban missiles substantially augmented Moscow's strength because now they had more missiles to strike America. Secretary McNamara contended it made no difference in strength if missiles came from Cuba or the Soviet Union. Unless the Soviets wanted to give the U.S. advance warning, they would have to time all missiles to hit the U.S. simultaneously.

ExCom members also differed on whether Khrushchev was concerned primarily about Berlin or Turkey. Berlin attracted the attention of McGeorge Bundy because it was the principal cause of U.S.—Soviet tensions during 1961 and the summer of 1962; thus, a Berlin settlement seemed to be a most reasonable Soviet motive. In contrast, Dean Rusk argued that the Turkish missile bases were the focus of Khrushchev's effort. Rusk observed that Khrushchev wanted Americans to feel the threat of nearby Cuban missiles just as the Soviet people felt the threat of U.S. missiles based in Turkey.[14]

As discussed previously (pages 15–17), some ExCom members believed Khrushchev was testing the American will to act in a crisis, an idea dismissed by later scholars. To the contrary, the ExCom never appears to have fully considered Soviet weaknesses which probably motivated their Cuban missile decision (see pages 17–30).

Political—Diplomatic Considerations

The ExCom devoted its primary attention to an American response which would secure the removal of Soviet missiles from Cuba. Although the ExCom gave its greatest attention to a military response, it did consider possible political—diplomatic responses. During the October 16 ExCom sessions, Secretary of State Rusk offered two diplomatic options. First, he suggested that the U.S. might act in conjunction with its NATO and OAS allies. Although ExCom members such as Vice President Lyndon Johnson doubted the value of these groups in pressuring Khrushchev to remove the Cuban missiles, Rusk questioned the wisdom of an American response without prior notification of its allies since a U.S. military attack on Cuba might cause the Soviet Union to retaliate in Europe or Latin America. Nevertheless, most ExCom members as well as President Kennedy believed the allies would not respond quickly enough to the threat. Once negotiations began, they feared the talks would drag on while the Soviets completed the site construction and made its Cuban—based missiles operational. Such a *fait accompli* would complicate any effort to remove the missiles.[15]

A second diplomatic proposal hatched by Rusk and Edwin Martin was to notify Castro that Khrushchev planned to trade Cuban bases for more vital Soviet objectives in Berlin and Turkey. If Castro believed this suggestion, the U.S. would achieve two purposes, removing the Soviet missiles and causing a Cuban—Soviet split. President Kennedy thought less of this plan than Rusk's initial idea and it was quickly dropped.[16] Later, the president complained to Charles Bohlen that he was disappointed about the unimaginative approaches to policy coming from the State Department.

In fact, Kennedy's meetings with Bohlen on October 16 and 17, provided another diplomatic proposal for the ExCom. By coincidence, Bohlen visited the president on October 16 prior to leaving for Paris to become Ambassador to France. Kennedy told Bohlen about the U—2 photos and suggested he attend the ExCom session on October 17.

As a result, Bohlen had an opportunity to urge strongly the use of diplomacy *before* taking military action against Cuba. In a memorandum, Bohlen suggested a private diplomatic approach to the Soviets in which Kennedy would say "we mean business," and demand that the missiles be removed. Bohlen contended that the air strike would not be the "neat, quick disposal of their bases as was suggested" but would lead to general war with Cuba. If the U.S. desired to invade Cuba, it should not initiate an attack without first getting support from its allies and formally declaring war. In this case, America could use its superior military power to defeat Cuba. Bohlen believed such action would be less likely to cause a world war than a secret air attack. Bohlen did not meet again with the ExCom but handed his October 18 memorandum to Dean Rusk.

Although Kennedy contemplated having Bohlen delay his trip to France, Bohlen left as scheduled because the White House did not want to change any routine that might alert Moscow to the fact that the U.S. had discovered the Soviet missile bases. The ExCom considered Bohlen's plan to contact Khrushchev but no one could devise a message which would avoid diplomatic wrangling while the Soviets completed their missile construction. Nevertheless, by October 18, the ExCom had turned away from support for an air strike to favor a low-level military response, the naval blockade.[17]

Following Bohlen's departure, Adlai Stevenson suffered particular abuse from Kennedy and his advisors because he suggested various diplomatic methods to solve the crisis through discussions with Moscow, either at the United Nations or the Organization of American States. After his suggestions for general diplomacy were dismissed by the ExCom, Stevenson asked the group to consider various negotiable positions such as trading Guantanamo or a Turkish missile base for the Cuban bases, exchanges which would avoid a military confrontation. Again, Stevenson was rebuked. According to Stevenson's biographer, John B. Martin, the president led the attack on Stevenson, arguing that this was not the time to consider negotiations; only after the Soviets yielded and removed their missiles could negotiations begin. The president's attitude prevailed in the ExCom, subjecting Stevenson both during and after the crisis to scorn as "too weak" to deal with Russia. On October 22, Kennedy asked John McCloy to join Stevenson at the United Nations to make certain the ambassador did not weaken.[18]

Roger Hilsman, one of Kennedy's ardent admirers, argues that diplomacy would have taken too long because the MRBMs might become operational by October 30, and the IRBMs by November 15. According to Ronald Steel (M-36), Hilsman overlooks the possibility that if Kennedy had given a strong diplomatic warning to Andrei Gromyko with whom the president met on October 18, there would have been from 12 to 27 days before the Soviet missiles could be used. Moscow would hardly attack with only MRBMs in place. Considering that the U.S.S.R. had only ten ICBMs at their home bases, their only effective strike before November 15 would have been against the NATO nations during diplomatic discussions about Cuba. From October 16 to 22, Steele argues, the operational status of the Cuban missiles should have had less effect than it did on Kennedy's choice of a diplomatic or military response.[19]

Although the ExCom, both on October 16 and after, considered diplomatic methods as a means of responding to the missile crisis, it gave its principal attention to examining various forms of a U.S. military response. For reasons tied closely to domestic politics, the president and the ExCom believed a military response was essential for both personal and national reasons. First, Kennedy's 1960 presidential campaign had denounced President Eisenhower's weakness toward Cuba and the Soviets; and, secondly, Kennedy's September 1962 reassurance policy included a pledge that he would do whatever was necessary to neutralize any "offensive" missiles found in Cuba.

During the 1960 political campaign, Kennedy and Democratic politicians had led the public to expect vigorous action against any communist threat. The Democrats' campaign had geared its foreign policy statements to allegations that Eisenhower had vacillated in his policies toward Castro and had permitted Moscow to achieve superiority in nuclear missiles. In contrast, Kennedy contended that he would reassert American power to regain the American position as the world's international leader.

Military Options Considered

While Kennedy's rhetoric presaged a strong U.S. reaction, the president's September promise to act against any offensive missiles was the most prominent reason why a military response seemed necessary after October 16. On at least two occasions during that day's ExCom session, the president made it clear that he had to remove the missiles. Kennedy and the ExCom believed the September statements had warned the Soviets not to construct MRBM bases in Cuba and that the American people would expect some type of military response. George Ball, who usually advocated moderation, stated the point most explicitly on October 16: "...as far as the American people are concerned, action means military action, period." As John C. Donovan's study of America's Cold War warriors indicates, in a crisis with communism,

U.S. politicians have usually preferred to err in being tough toward the Soviet Union.[20]

In the context of the ExCom's domestic political views, the group's sessions, not surprisingly, focused on either a surgical air strike, a broad air strike, an air strike plus a large scale U.S. invasion of Cuba, or a naval blockade. As they dissected these military alternatives, the ExCom divided into two groups which Stewart Alsop (B—1) dubbed the "hawks" and the "doves." Both groups favored a military response: the "hawks" advocating a secret and massive air attack and invasion of Cuba; the "doves" preferring the less—aggressive naval quarantine.

Although initially some type of air strike had the ExCom's general support, this option eventually lost to the idea of a naval quarantine for three reasons: 1) the Air Force's insistence on a massive, not a surgical strike; 2) the "Pearl Harbor" analogy; and 3) the belief that the quarantine did not preclude an air strike or invasion if the blockade failed.

First, the secret air strike option against Cuba lost some of its ExCom adherents because the Air Force insisted on a massive air attack on Cuba rather than a limited strike designed to eliminate the missile bases. From the outset of the October 16 meetings, McNamara and General Taylor argued that the air attack must be against the missile sites "plus the airfields, plus the aircraft which may not be in the airfields but hidden by that time, plus any potential nuclear storage sites." An air and sea invasion might also be necessary because the Joint Chiefs of Staff wanted the attacks to succeed "100 percent just as far" as possible.

Vice President Lyndon B. Johnson fully supported Taylor. Although not saying much during the ExCom sessions, Johnson delivered an ardent hawkish tirade on October 16. He not only rejected Rusk's notions of relying on allies but did not want to notify Congress in advance of an air strike. Johnson believed Americans were fearful and "they're unsure, and we're getting divided...." Thus Johnson wanted the U.S. to attack and to "stop the planes, stop the ships, stop the submarines and everything else... and then stop them from coming in."[21]

The option of a massive air attack was unsatisfactory to several ExCom members. In particular, McGeorge Bundy thought one limited surgical strike against the Soviet's offensive missile bases was all that was necessary. The limited strike would achieve America's basic goal and cause less risk of nuclear retaliation by the Soviet Union. A general strike would kill many Soviet and Cuban personnel, deaths which would require the Kremlin to respond in kind.[22]

On the advice of the hawkish Chief of the Strategic Air Command, General Curtis LeMay, General Taylor and the Joint Chiefs overplayed their hand. When Dean Acheson (M−46) was called in for consultation with the ExCom on October 17, he strongly favored a surgical air strike but could not accept the risks involved in a massive strike. Acheson believed the surgical strike would eliminate the offensive missile bases, minimize civilian casualties and be more likely to prevent a large scale nuclear war with the Soviet Union.[23]

To LeMay, however, the surgical air strike would be difficult because of the SAMs. More important, this strike would not be sufficient to eliminate the Russian threat in Cuba. LeMay claimed the selective air strike had only a 90% chance of total success and could not guarantee achievement of the necessary military objective; that is, the elimination of all Soviet threats in Cuba. LeMay sought both a massive air strike and a U.S. ground invasion to overthrow communism in Cuba and remove all Soviet bases from the island.

President Kennedy and other ExCom members were amazed that the military chiefs did not take into account the Soviet reaction to a devastating attack that would kill many Soviet soldiers as well as Cuban citizens and soldiers. LeMay assured the president that "there will be no [Soviet] reactions." Theodore Sorensen reports that during one verbal exchange, an unidentified "hawk" admitted the Soviet Union would probably respond to an American attack by knocking out a U.S. base in Turkey. The president asked: "What will we do then?" The member responded: "Under our NATO treaty, we'd be obligated to knock out a base in the Soviet Union." To Kennedy's subsequent question, "What will they do then?", the response was "Why, then we hope everyone will cool down and want to talk."[24]

By focusing on the costs and risks of a massive air attack, such exchanges persuaded some ExCom members to oppose an air attack, while others rejected Taylor's proposals because of the "Pearl Harbor" analogy. Although Robert Kennedy has become best known for his opposition to a surprise air attack on Cuba because it would be compared to the Japanese attack on Hawaii in 1941, the transcripts of the October 16 ExCom meetings indicate George Ball first mentioned Pearl Harbor. Speaking in favor of the blockade, Ball said: "This, uh, come in there on Pearl Harbor [sic] just frightens the hell out of me as to what's going beyond...what happens beyond that. You go in there with a surprise attack. You put out all the missiles. This isn't the *end.* This is the beginning, I think."

In his memoirs, Robert Kennedy said that during the meeting, he had passed a note to the president which said, "I now know how Tojo felt when he was planning Pearl Harbor."[25] Whether or not Ball saw this note, the ExCom's talk about a surprise air attack on Cuba must have conjured up December 7, 1941, in the minds of many of the participants. The president's brother had also asked the ExCom how the U.S. would react if the Soviets bombed Berlin or West Germany?

Later on Friday, October 19, when the Joint Chiefs of Staff supported by Dean Acheson argued strongly for a secret air strike, Robert Kennedy openly related such action to Pearl Harbor and mentioned the moral burden the U.S. would bear afterward. The U.S. simply was not "that kind of country," he said.[26]

The problem of an attack without warning was complicated by the hawks belief that an advance warning would be hazardous and would enable the Soviets to stall for time to make all their missiles operational. Various scenarios which included either a warning or an "immediate" ultimatum to Moscow seemed to risk failure. Apparently, some ExCom "hawks" feared a warning would open the diplomatic channels which they considered a sign of weakness.

Although Dean Acheson opposed the Pearl Harbor analogy as "false and perjorative," several ExCom members had become concerned by the moral and humanitarian implications of a secret U.S. air attack on Cuba. The October 16 transcript indicates that such considerations led Bundy, McNamara, and Ball to suggest consideration of the naval blockade near the end of the first two ExCom sessions. Following a day of thought and discussion about U.S. military options, these three ExCom members urged the group to consider the post−crisis implications of an American attack on Cuba. According to McNamara, "...the most important thing we need to do is this appraisal of the world *after* any one of these situations."

Beginning with his concern for the post−attack consequences, McNamara asked, rhetorically, if there really was a military problem. He concluded there was not. The problem, he said, was "...if Cuba should possess a capacity to carry out offensive actions against the U.S., the U.S. would act." How should the U.S. act about the missiles? "Well, we want to act to prevent their use." One action the U.S. could undertake would be open surveillance and a blockade of offensive weapons headed for Cuba. We would warn them that if we found any indication that the missiles will be used, "...we will respond not only against Cuba, but we will respond directly against the Soviet Union with . . . a full nuclear strike."

This portion of the October 16 transcript concluded: "McNamara: Now this alternative doesn't seem to be a very acceptable one, but wait until you work on the others. Bundy: That's right. (Laughter)."[27] The laughter relieved the tension after the ExCom members had considered and stepped away from recommending a surprise air attack on Cuba. The final decision on the blockade did not come until October 20, however.

On October 18, further consideration of the naval blockade disclosed its principal advantage; that is, the blockade could be announced as an initial response which could be followed by stronger military action if Khrushchev did not remove the Soviet missiles from Cuba. Exactly what America's second step would be could remain open. The U.S. air strike could be ordered if the Soviets did not remove their missiles. Although the element of total surprise would be lost, the U.S. would not have to announce the precise method, time and place of attack. Thus, the blockade *plus* the threat of escalating military action would give the Soviet Union time to decide on its move but not enough time to stall until the bases became operational.

The Blockade Decision

Although Sorensen asserts that President Kennedy had made up his mind by Thursday, October 18, to use the blockade, the president waited until October 20, after the ExCom voted 11 to 6 to recommend the blockade, before telling the group his preference. During the interim, the president had further briefings on the air strike with the Joint Chiefs and Air Force officers before finalizing his decision for the blockade on October 21.[28]

The Saturday decision gave Kennedy's administration four days to prepare the details of the blockade while the U.S. military continued their preparations in the event the blockade failed to persuade Khrushchev to remove the missile. In addition, the State Department contacted NATO and the OAS members, and the president drafted his television speech to the American people for Monday, October 22. The speech would inform the nation of the Soviet–Cuban deception and announce the U.S. naval blockade designed to eliminate this threat to the Western Hemisphere.

The president's message also warned Moscow and Havana that the U.S. would escalate its military action if the blockade did not persuade Khrushchev to remove Soviet missiles from Cuba. Therefore, from October 22 to 28, two Soviet decisions would be critical: (1) how to repond to the U.S. naval blockade, and (2) what to do with their missiles in Cuba in order to avoid a complete military−diplomatic setback. Kennady had selected a firm but flexible response. He hoped the Soviet leaders could also be flexible and pull their missiles out of Cuba, and area where their lack of conventional military strength put them at a decided disadvantage.

NOTES

1. Senator Keating, *Congressional Record*, 88th Cong. 2d Sess., vol. 108, 18359−18361.

2. For insight into the "crisis of September 1962," see issues of *New York Times*, Aug. 15 to Oct. 14. Almost each day, some report on Cuban affairs dealt with demonstrations, exile attacks or other material cited in this study.

3. George W. Johnson, ed., (New York: Coleman Enterprises, 1978), 385.

4. George and Smoke, *Deterrence*, 466−472.

5. *ExCom Sess. Oct. 16*, second session, 36.

6. Hilsman, *To Move A Nation*, 167−170.

7. On the "intelligence gap," see *ibid.*, 159−192; George and Smoke, *Deterrence*, 472−491; Hilsman and Ronald Steel, "An Exchange of Views," 17−21; Klaus Knorr, "Fortune on National Intelligence Estimates: The Case of the Cuban Missile Crisis," *World Politics* 16 (Apr. 1964), 455−467.

8. Arthur Krock, *Memoirs* (New York: Funk & Wagnalls, 1968), 378–80; Allison, *Essence of Decision*, 190–192; Phillipe de Vasjoli, "So Much Has Been Swept Under the Rug," *Life* (Apr. 26, 1968), 35. Vasjoli's removal from the French secret service by President DeGaulle has cast doubt on the veracity of his memoir.

9. On Kennedy's request to call up reservists, see *New York Times*, Sept. 8, 1962, p. 1; on the Congressional resolution, see *ibid.*, Sept. 20, pp. 14, 32, and Sept. 21, p. 1.

10. U.S. Congress, Senate, Committee on Armed Services, Preparedness Investigating Subcommittee, *Interim Report on Cuban Military Build-up*, 88th Cong., 1st Sess., (Washington, DC: GPO, 1968), 9; Elie Abel, *The Missile Crisis* (New York: Praeger, 1966), 26ff.

11. CIA reports of October 23 thru 28, 1962, ExCom National Security Files, JFK Library, Boxes 315–316. CIA reports for October 1962 are available on microfilm; see Paul Kesaris, ed., "CIA Research Reports: Latin America, 1946–1976." (Frederick, MD: University Publications, 1982). Portions of the CIA reports of October 21, 25, 26, are in Dan Caldwell, *Missiles in Cuba: A Decision-Making Game* (New York: Learning Resources in International Studies, 1979), 5–20.

12. Allison, *Essence of Decision*, 109–113.

13. The ExCom was constituted officially on October 22, 1962, by NSAM 196. In addition to the members cited here, other persons attended some ExCom meetings, see Theodore Sorensen, *Kennedy* (New York: Harper & Row, 1965), 674–675.

14. *ExCom Sess. Oct. 16*, statements of Maxwell Taylor, first sess., 13 and second sess., 12–13; of U. Alexis Johnson, second sess., 26–27; of McNamara and Bundy, second sess., 12–13; of J.F. Kennedy, second sess., 13–15. On Berlin and Turkey, see Rusk and Bundy statements, first sess., 15–16; Ball statement, second sess., 25–26; Rusk and J.F. Kennedy statements, first sess., 14–15.

15. *Ibid.*, statements of Rusk, first sess., 8–11; of Dillon and J.F. Kennedy, first sess., 16–17; of Taylor, second session, 36; of Lyndon Johnson, first sess., 20–21.

16. *Ibid.*, Rusk and Martin statements, second session, 5–7.

17. Charles Bohlen, *Witness to History, 1929–1969* (New York: Norton, 1973), 488–492. Bohlen appears to be incorrect in saying the

54 The Missile Crisis

Kennedy meeting was on October 17. The ExCom recording transcript indicates the president remarked he had shown Bohlen U−2 photos on October 16. *ExCom sess. Oct. 16.*, first sess. 28.

18. John B. Martin, *Adlai Stevenson and the World* (Garden City, NY: Doubleday, 1972,) 702−748.

19. Steel, "Endgame," 15−22; Hilsman and Steel, "An Exchange of Views," 37−38. Sorensen says Kennedy abandoned diplomatic options from the outset, *Kennedy*, 683.

20. *ExCom Sess. Oct. 16*, George Ball statement, second sess., 48; John C. Donovan, *The Cold Warriors* Lexington, MA: D.C. Heath, 1974), 150−151, 259−272.

21. *ExCom Sess., Oct. 16*, McNamara and Taylor statements, first sess., 11−14, 17−18 and second sess., 7−10, 16−19; Lyndon Johnson statment, first sess., 20−21.

22. *Ibid.*, Bundy statements, first sess., 17, 25−28; second sess., 18, 43.

23. Dean Acheson, "Dean Acheson's Version of Robert Kennedy's Version of the Cuban Missile Affair: Homage to Plain Dumb Luck," *Esquire* 71 (Feb. 1969), 44, 76.

24. Robert Kennedy, *Thirteen Days*, 36; Abel, *Missile Crisis*, 78−81; Sorensen, *Kennedy*, 684−692.

25. R. Kennedy, *Thirteen Days*, 31. Ball's statement on Pearl Harbor is in *ExCom Sess. Oct. 16*, second session, 49. Schlesinger, *RFK*, indicates the Tojo note was passed to Sorensen, not the president, p. 1018, fn. 33.

26. R. Kennedy, *Thirteen Days*, 49.

27. *ExCom Sess. Oct. 16*, statements of R. Kennedy, first sess., 21; J.F. Kennedy, second sess., 23−25; McNamara and Bundy, second sess., 22, 40−41, 45−47.

28. Allison, *Essence of Decision*, 60−61; Sorensen, *Kennedy*, 688. For President Kennedy's October 27, 1962 message to Khrushchev, see J.F. Kennedy, *Public Papers−1962*, 813−814.

IV

JFK'S Blockade Strategy, October 22–28

While Kennedy and his advisors took four days to decide on the naval blockade, they needed two more days to prepare for the public disclosure that Soviet missiles had been discovered in Cuba and that the U.S. planned to blockade the sea routes between Russia and Cuba. The television speech had to be readied, the armed forces had to be alerted and positioned, and U.S. diplomats had to inform U.S. allies and to prepare for emergency sessions of the OAS and U.N. Security Council. Not least of all, Congressional leaders had to be briefed before the Monday night speech.

PREPARATIONS TO ANNOUNCE THE BLOCKADE

The opportunity to inform allies was an added *plus* for the quarantine option. In the OAS, among its European allies, and within the Asia–African bloc in the United Nations, American diplomats gained time to rally world opinion against the Soviet action, opinion which would have been sacrificed by the unannounced air strike option.

Beginning on Monday, October 22, State Department representatives contacted allied embassies in Washington. Special meetings were arranged with America's major European allies. Dean Acheson flew to Europe to explain the decisions to French President Charles DeGaulle and West German Chancellor Konrad Adenauer. On his way, Acheson stopped in London to explain Kennedy's actions to U.S. Ambassador David Bruce, who informed Prime Minister Macmillan. John Diefenbaker, Canada's Prime Minister was contacted personally and agreed to help convince other nations that the U.S. acted correctly.[1]

As these personal contacts continued, plans were made to convene an emergency OAS session and a UN Security Council meeting. Secretary of State Rusk and Edwin Martin of the Latin American bureau of the State Department contacted Latin American diplomats in

Range of Soviet Missiles

Washington and called a Tuesday morning OAS meeting. Arthur Schlesinger, Jr., assisted Adlai Stevenson in preparing his brief for the UN Security Council, a case designed to demonstrate Soviet duplicity in sending nuclear arms to Cuba.

While the diplomats sought backing for the low-level military response, the Defense Department finalized plans to set up the blockade and to respond with greater force if the blockade failed. U.S. missile crews went on alert beginning Monday, October 22; 200,000 troops moved into Florida in case a Cuban invasion became necessary; B-52 bombers of the Strategic Air Command were dispersed to air fields in Florida and other Southern states; 14,000 Air Force reserve pilots rushed to duty and prepared to fly military transport planes; the First Armoured Division began its move from Texas to Georgia; and the navy deployed 180 ships to the Caribbean area and strengthened its base defenses at Guantanamo.

These military preparations would enable the U.S. to quickly escalate the level of its military action. In America's open society, news of these movements became obvious not only to Americans but to the Soviet Union. Khrushchev referred to these military preparations in his messages to Kennedy after October 22 and, later, in his report on the crisis to the Supreme Council of the Soviet Union.

BLOCKADE INCREASES SOVIET--AMERICAN TENSIONS

The week from October 22 to 28 was filled with moments of tense waiting and dramatic decisions before the final deal was struck ending the Cuban missile crisis. Those events which most directly influenced Chairman Khrushchev's and President Kennedy's decision to make a deal on October 28 are reconstructed here from the memoirs of such participants as Robert Kennedy and Theodore Sorensen as well as material from Congressional hearings and partly declassified data from the John F. Kennedy Library and Lyndon B. Johnson Library.

Monday: October 22

Before his television address, President Kennedy met with Congressional leaders while Secretary of State Rusk visited Soviet Ambassador Dobrynin. After learning about the intended U.S. blockade, Dobrynin left the State Department in what reporters described as a "considerably shaken" condition. Many analysts believe the Ambassador did not know exactly what his government was doing in Cuba because of the secrecy decreed in Moscow. There is evidence that the Soviet's KGB man in Washington, Alexander Fomin, was the one kept up−to−date on Cuban events. Fomin would enter into the week's events on Friday.

President Kennedy's 5:00 p.m. meeting with Congressional leaders prompted dissenting opinion from those legislators who desired a stronger military response. Two leading Senate Democrats, Richard Russell of Georgia and J. William Fulbright of Arkansas, believed there should be an air strike or invasion as soon as possible. Although their reactions resembled the initial reaction of the ExCom and the president on October 16, Kennedy became angry with their militant attitude. He defended his decision, pointing out that an all−out nuclear war could result from any miscalculation. If Soviet soldiers were killed and the Russians responded in kind, millions of Americans would die in minutes and many more deaths might occur before the destruction stopped. Whether convinced or not, the Congressmen would support the president during the next week.[2]

The long session with the Congressmen left Kennedy little time before his TV address at 7:00 p.m. His nationwide speech declared that continued surveillance of Soviet activity in Cuba had revealed offensive nuclear missile sites under construction in Cuba which threatened American security. The MRBM missile's range enabled them to strike Washington, D.C., the Panama Canal, Mexico City, and other cities in the southeast U.S., Central America and Caribbean. After Russia's IRBMs became operational, they could strike as far north as Hudson's Bay and as far south as Lima, Peru.

Because of this extraordinary Soviet threat to the Western Hemisphere, President Kennedy reported he had ordered the "following *initial* steps to be taken immediately."

1. The quarantine of all offensive military equipment being shipped to Cuba from whatever nation or port, but the necessities of life would not be stopped.

2. The continued, close surveillance of Cuba and its military build up. Should the Soviet offensive construction continue, further action would be justified. He trusted, however, that "in the interest of both the Cuban people and Soviet technicians at the sites, the hazards to all concerned of continuing this threat will be recognized."

3. Any missile launched from Cuba against the Western Hemisphere should be regarded as an attack by the Soviets on the United States, "requiring a full retaliatory response upon the Soviet Union."

4. Guantanamo would be reinforced and dependents of U.S. personnel evacuated.

5. The U.S. would call for an immediate OAS meeting to consider the threat and to support all necessary action. Our other world allies would be contacted to gain their backing.

6. The U.S. would request an emergency session of the U.N. Security Council to act on the Soviet threat to peace. It would ask for the dismantling and withdrawal of "all offensive weapons in Cuba, under supervision of U.N. observers before the quarantine can be lifted."

7. The president would call on Chairman Khrushchev to halt this provocative threat to peace and join in an effort to end the perilous arms race. He could "move the world back from the abyss of destruction" by returning the missiles to Soviet territory and by refraining from actions that might deepen the crisis.

Finally, the president called on the Cuban people to rise up and overthrow their tyrannical government so that Cuba would become a free society. He warned America that the path he had chosen was full of hazards but was consistent with our nation's character, courage, and commitment. The U.S. could not submit or surrender if we were to achieve "peace and freedom" in this hemisphere and around the world.[3]

The president's speech combined the immediate imposition of the quarantine with a threat that additional U.S. action could follow. He also sought to rally OAS and world opinion to support the "quarantine," a less bellicose word for the blockade.

Tuesday: October 23

This was probably the most relaxed day in Washington between October 16 and 29, 1962. Kennedy's decision had been announced, and the quarantine would not become operative until 10:00 a.m. on Wednesday. However, important diplomatic efforts highlighted the day's activity.

The most critical diplomatic development was the OAS's unanimous vote to support JFK's quarantine. Secretary Rusk and Edwin Martin had prepared well for the Tuesday morning OAS session. During the Punte del Este conference in February 1962, six Latin American nations, including Mexico, Argentina, Brazil, and Chile, had rejected the U.S. proposal to end all OAS relations with Castro's Cuba. In contrast, at the October 23 meeting, the OAS unanimously approved two of the three votes taken on the U.S. resolution regarding the missiles in Cuba.

As F. Parkinson's study (Q–10) indicates, the OAS council unanimously accepted the essential parts of the U.S. resolution on Cuba although three nations abstained on the most aggressive portion of the proposal. The two critical sections called for the withdrawal of all Soviet offensive weapons from Cuba and stated that the OAS would inform the United Nations about its regional activity under the UN charter. These sections of the resolution enabled the U.S. to base the naval blockade on the legal argument that the OAS was the security group responsible for the Caribbean area. Under the UN Charter, regional groups could act in their area but were responsible for reporting to the New York UN headquarters.

On the third OAS vote, Bolivia, Brazil, and Mexico abstained on the section of the U.S. resolution calling for individual and collective action, including use of armed forces, to halt the entry of weapons, and to prevent them from becoming an active threat to the Western Hemisphere. Each of the three nations had different reasons for abstaining. Mexico's abstention was the most significant because it sympathized with Cuba more than other OAS nations. President Lopez Mateos approved the first two resolutions because he opposed the introduction of nuclear weapons in Latin America. His nation abstained on the third vote because it allowed too much latitude for unilateral U.S. action during the crisis.

Following the OAS vote, the Pentagon called on OAS member nations to send ships to join the Cuban blockade. The Latin American reaction disappointed Washington. The question went to the OAS where it was discussed until November 5. By the time the OAS approved the request, the blockade was in a passive mode awaiting Russia's full compliance with its October 28 deal with Kennedy. The OAS debate and vote revealed little trust in American leadership. Brazil, Bolivia and Mexico disliked the proposal and abstained on the measure. The Inter—American Quarantine Force set up on November 9 included naval vessels only from Argentina, Honduras and Peru. Six other Caribbean States offered cooperation but no ships. Nevertheless, Secretary Rusk had gained the crucial "removal of weapons" vote from the OAS, a vote which was necessary in justifying the American case before the U.N. Security Council.[4]

Following the OAS session, President Kennedy initiated two contacts with Soviet officials on October 23. He sent Khrushchev a personal note and asked his brother Robert to talk with Ambassador Dobrynin. In his letter to Khrushchev, the president explained that since the OAS action gave legal sanction to the naval quarantine, he hoped the U.S.S.R. would observe the blockade so that the U.S. would not have to fire on a Soviet ship. He asked the Soviet Chairman to act prudently and not to "allow events to make the situation more difficult to control than it is." Generally, Kennedy's message reflected a conciliatory tone in contrast to his more bellicose television speech.

Robert Kennedy's contact with Ambassador Dobrynin had little consequence. Kennedy's intention was to let Dobrynin realize that the strong military level response to the news of Soviet offensive missiles resulted because of Soviet duplicity about its Cuban plans during September. Dobrynin claimed he was ignorant of Moscow's plans for Cuba, having been told by Khrushchev that there were no such missiles. When asked what the Russian reaction to the quarantine would be, Dobrynin said that to his best knowledge the Soviet ships would go through to Cuba. When Robert reported this statement to his brother, the president did not seem greatly disturbed. Perhaps, as later analysts concluded, the Kennedys realized that Dobrynin's view on the blockade was unimportant, since, similarly, Americans at the Moscow embassy were not up—to—date on White House decisions. The difficulty of rapid high—level communication became obvious to Kennedy and Khrushchev during October 1962. (As a result, one outcome of the missile crisis was the establishment of a direct "hot—line" between the Kremlin and the White House.)[5]

Wednesday To Friday Morning: October 24–26

Events from Wednesday until noon Friday did not clarify Soviet intentions regarding the Cuban missiles. During the first two days of the blockade, both Kennedy and Khrushchev acted cautiously to avoid a clash or to make statements which might be irrevocable or provocative.

According to the accounts by Sorensen and Abel, the president took steps to be certain that he managed the naval blockade by methods which would give the Soviet leaders time to see, think and, hopefully, withdraw their ships. Later accounts resulted in disputes regarding the U.S. Navy's role in carrying out presidential orders. Although Allison concluded that the navy did not properly follow the president's orders, Dan Caldwell's study (M–51) of navy ship logs confirmed Admiral George Anderson's (M–47) contention that the navy, in fact, followed the president's orders.

President Kennedy's use of direct communication with commanders aboard the navy's destroyers allowed him to control the navy's implementation of the quarantine. During the four days of crisis, the president obtained data about each Russian ship approaching the blockade line and used the information to determine which vessels should be confronted and inspected by U.S. Navy officers and which should be permitted to pass—by the quarantine.[6]

At the White House, the first tense moments occurred during the half–hour following the beginning of the quarantine at 10:00 a.m. on Wednesday, October 24. Within 15 minutes, two Soviet ships, the *Gargarin* and the *Komiles,* would reach the blockade line. As Kennedy and his staff waited anxiously for the outcome, a report that a Soviet submarine moved into position between the two ships added to their anxiety. Not until 10:25, could the White House staff relax. A messenger brought news that the Russian ships had stopped dead in the water. At 10:32, this report was confirmed with the additional information that fourteen Soviet ships in the vicinity of the blockade had either stopped or turned back toward their home ports. Khrushchev had decided not to challenge the quarantine.

Nevertheless, the Soviet Union did not officially acknowledge its acceptance of the blockade while, in Cuba, U–2 flights indicated that missile site construction was continuing. Pending Moscow's official acceptance of the quarantine, the U.S. Navy had to stop and board a Soviet ship in order to establish the blockade's full authority. President Kennedy decided to choose carefully which ship the navy would board.

On Thursday, the president permitted a Soviet tanker, the *Bucharest*, to pass through the blockade after identifying itself. Kennedy had agreed that the necessities of life could pass through and it appeared that the ship carried only oil. Therefore, the president let it pass but told the navy to follow and observe it.

At 7 a.m. Friday, the navy boarded the ship selected by the president. The ship was the *Marcula*, a Lebanese registered freighter under Panamanian and Greek ownership, leased to the Soviet Union. Because it was not Soviet-owned, the choice symbolized a less bellicose approach than the search of a Soviet vessel. The Friday morning search went smoothly. After U.S. naval officers found no weapons on board, the *Marcula* proceeded to Cuba.

Other encounters between Soviet and American naval vessels went equally well from the U.S. perspective. President Kennedy had feared that an encounter with Soviet submarines might be a problem. The U.S. Navy was proud of the Anti-Submarine Warfare (ASW) methods it had developed over the years. Following the crisis, Chief of Naval Operations Admiral George Anderson boasted that during the Cuban missile crisis the ASW conducted its most extensive and productive anti-submarine operations since World War II. Naval destroyers located and followed all Soviet submarines within 600 miles of the U.S. mainland. They even forced several Soviet submarines to surface without incurring the incident the president feared.[7]

Before Friday noon, although the Soviet ships had not challenged the quarantine, Khrushchev had not indicated his willingness to remove the missiles from Cuba. On October 23 and 25, the Soviet Chairman answered two earlier Kennedy letters but his responses contained only accusations and threats, which also were careful not to antagonize the Americans. On October 24, Khrushchev endorsed Bertrand Russell's proposal for a summit meeting with Kennedy. Kennedy rejected the British philosopher's request, observing that Russell's message sought to conciliate the burglar while critizing the one who had caught the felon.

Prior to noon on Friday, there were a few favorable signals from Moscow of which W. Averell Harriman sought to apprise the president. A long-time diplomate and Soviet expert who Secretary Rusk's followers at the State Department pointedly ignored, Harriman had telephoned Sorensen who was in New York on October 24. Harriman had detected evidence indicating Khrushchev was trying to get off the hook: his acceptance of Russell's suggestion for a summit meeting; his alternately amiable and hostile Moscow meeting with U.S. businessman

William Knox of Westinghouse; his publicized visit with American singer Jerome Hines who was on a concert tour in Moscow; and the Soviet failure to challenge the blockade. Kennedy, Harriman said, should not get tougher but should help Khrushchev find a way to retreat. Sorensen called the President and persuaded Kennedy to talk by telephone with Harriman. Although not certain, Sorensen believes Harriman influenced the president to instruct Ambassador Stevenson to explore means for removing the Cuban missiles with UN Secretary General U Thant and the Soviet UN Ambassador Valerian Zorin.[8]

During the Thursday session of the UN Security Council, Ambassador Stevenson performed well. During his presentation, Stevenson prodded Zorin to confirm or deny that there were Soviet missiles in Cuba. Zorin refused to answer, saying "I am not in an American court of law." Stevenson continued:

> You are in the courtroom of world opinion. You have denied they exist, and I want to know if I understand you correctly.
>
> I am prepared to wait until hell freezes over if that's your decision. And I am also prepared to present the evidence in this room—
> —now![9]

Ambassador Stevenson then displayed enlargements of the U−2 photos to the council, showing proof of the existence of Soviet missiles in Cuba. The episode won wide−spread support for the U.S. among neutral nations in the Asian−African bloc while it damaged the Soviet image as a peace−maker. Nevertheless, Zorin vetoed the UN resolution against Soviet's actions in Cuba. Furthermore, his contacts with Stevenson about removing the missiles achieved nothing until October 28, following Khrushchev's announcement of the decision to withdraw the missiles.

By Friday morning events favored United States policy, yet Moscow had not responded to the critical issue: would the missiles be removed from Cuba? Having no answer and knowing from U−2 photos that missile construction activity had speeded−up since Monday, Kennedy and the ExCom met on Friday morning to consider escalating the American response with an air strike and invasion of Cuba. The Joint Chiefs of Staff insisted that further delay would permit the Soviets to make all their missiles operational. Already, they argued, both the massive air strike and an invasion would result in greater casualties than a secret attack on October 22 would have caused. Consequently Friday morning, the president prepared to escalate the American response by ordering a program to organize a civil government in Cuba after the invasion. By noontime Friday, an escalation of the U.S. military response seemed imminent.

Friday Afternoon: October 26

On Friday afternoon, as anxiety was mounting at the White House, Kennedy received two reports indicating Khrushchev might remove the missiles. The first positive sign came about 3 p.m., through an unusual route: a verbal message to John Scali, the ABC news correspondent at the State Department, from Alexander Fomin, the Soviet's KGB agent in Washington. Telephoning Scali at 1:30 p.m., Fomin asked to lunch with Scali at the Occidental Restaurant. At their meeting, Fomin told Scali he feared war would break out. He asked if Scali thought America would promise not to invade Cuba if Khrushchev promised to remove the Soviet missiles from Cuba. Fomin wanted Scali to contact his State Department friends and discover the U.S. reaction to the question. Giving Scali his embassy phone number, he urged haste: "This is of vital importance."

Rushing to the State Department building, Scali informed Roger Hilsman of Fomin's question and Hilsman went to Secretary Rusk. Considering the source and substance of Scali's news, Rusk contacted the White House. Following an informal meeting to discuss Fomin's message, Kennedy approved a positive response for Fomin. Secretary of State Rusk informed Scali that the U.S. saw possibilities in Fomin's suggestion. Rusk added that the agreement Fomin offered could be worked out at the United Nations by Stevenson, Zorin and U Thant. Finally, Rusk emphasized that Scali should tell Fomin the "time is very urgent" and that the Russians must make their offer in not more than two days. Scali conveyed this information to Fomin immediately, and the Russian assured him he would inform Moscow.[10]

At 6 p.m., the Scali–Fomin exchange appeared to be verified when the State Department received a ten-page letter from Khrushchev via the U.S. Embassy in Moscow. The Soviet leader's note opened with an emotional description of the death, destruction, and anarchy which a nuclear war would bring. This, he said, must be avoided. If war began, "it would not be in our power to stop it, for such is the logic of war." Then in a crucial paragraph, Khrushchev stated:

> If the assurances were given by the President and the government of the United States that the USA itself would not participate in an

attack on Cuba and would restrain others from actions of this sort, if you would recall your fleet, this would immediately change everything. I am not speaking for Fidel Castro, but I think he and the government of Cuba, evidently, would declare demobilization and would appeal to the people to get down to peaceful labor. Then, too, the question of armaments would disappear, since, if there were no threat, then armaments are a burden to every people. Then, too, the question of the destruction, not only of the armaments which you call offensive, but of all other armaments as well, would look different.[11]

When the State Department examined Khrushchev's lengthy message, Secretary of State Rusk and Roger Hilsman were elated. Arriving just after the Fomin–Scali exchange, they assumed that the two contacts were "clearly related." According to Hilsman, Secretary Rusk told Scali: "John, you have served your country well. Remember when you report this--that eyeball to eyeball, they blinked first."[12]

Rusk and Hilsman also notified the president who reviewed the Khrushchev message with his brother and Sorensen. Although a decision on what seemed to be the Fomin–Khrushchev proposal was delayed until the State Department's Bureau of Intelligence and Research could analyze the letter and report to the ExCom on Saturday at 10:00 a.m., Khrushchev's letter relieved tension in Rusk's office and the White House. Robert Kennedy later reported that the president seemed "hopeful that our efforts might possibly be successful."[13]

On the evening of October 26, Khruschev's letter and the Fomin–Scali exchange seemed to have resulted in a possible deal to end the crisis. Rusk, Hilsman, and apparently the Kennedy brothers thought Khrushchev had offered to withdraw the Cuban missiles if the president pledged that the U.S. would not invade Cuba. In 1981, John Scherer's (P-12) analysis of the Khrushchev letter disputed the interpretation reached by the Kennedy administration on October 26-27, 1962. Scherer believed, for example, that the paragraph quoted above, required President Kennedy to take the first step in giving "assurances" and to "recall your fleet." Scherer's view was not considered in 1962, however. The prevailing belief of those who read Khrushchev's letter on Friday night and Saturday morning was that Khrushchev had offered to trade the missiles for a no-invasion pledge. Subsequently, Friday night's apparent optimism raised the ExCom's expectations to nearly tragic heights. On Saturday morning, when a second Khrushchev message, which appeared to withdraw his Friday concession, arrived in Washington about the same time that a Soviet SAM shot down a U-2 plane over Cuba, the missile crisis quickly moved to the brink of nuclear war.[14]

Saturday: October 27

On this day, the United States came closer to unleashing an air attack on Cuba than at any time during the crisis. Fortunately, the "hawks" were again brushed off and a last attempt was made to explore Khrushchev's proposals for Cuba. Two events had reduced the hopefulness of Friday evening to a near disaster on Saturday.

Initially, at 10:17 on Saturday morning, the White House received another letter from Khrushchev which appeared to differ significantly from his Friday note and bore the apparent imprint of the Soviet Foreign Office. The second letter stated the U.S. must remove its intermediate range Jupiter missiles from Turkey in addition to pledging not to invade Cuba. Although the promise not to invade seemed alright, neither the ExCom nor JFK wanted to remove the Turkish missiles under duress.

Actually, the Turkish missiles added little to the U.S.'s strategic deterrence program. The problem was that the missiles represented a U.S. pledge to NATO. The ExCom feared that any agreement to remove them would damage U.S. credibility as a world power and a NATO ally. The Jupiter missile bases originated during the Eisenhower Administration as one response to Sputnik and the much-publicized "missile-gap" episode. The Jupiter was a liquid fuel missile which had become obsolete when the second generation of solid fuel missiles became available. Neverthless, when the Jupiters had been offered to NATO nations in 1957, Turkey and Italy agreed to base them on their territory and, in 1959, an agreement to deploy them was finalized.

The U.S. delayed the deployment of the Jupiter missiles until Kennedy decided to deploy them during the summer of 1961. This decision followed Kennedy's failure at the Vienna Summit Conference to get Khrushchev to settle such issues as Berlin or Laos. The missiles did not become operational in Turkey until July 1962, by which time the Kennedy Administration was already seeking some way to persuade the Turkish government to withdraw them or exchange them for more up-to-date Polaris submarine bases.

As Barton Bernstein (F−2) has substantiated from recently released records and Kennedy Library files, JFK was not surprised to know the missiles were in Turkey as earlier accounts by Robert Kennedy, Hilsman, and Abel alleged. President Kennedy had, on August 23, ordered a feasibility study on removing the missiles but he had not ordered their removal. Throughout the ExCom sessions from October 16 to 27, the possibility of withdrawing the Turkish missiles had been discussed. Both the U.S. Ambassador to Turkey, Raymond Hare, and the U.S. NATO Ambassador, Thomas Finletter, informed ExCom that trading the Turkish missiles for Cuban missiles would cause difficulty in Europe. However, as Bernstein indicates, neither Hare nor Finletter were being asked, as President Kennedy was, to choose between a nuclear war or the Turkish missile bases. Nevertheless, on Saturday October 28, ExCom and Kennedy concurred with the ambassadors and initially elected to attack Cuba rather than agree to remove the Jupiter missiles from Turkey.[15]

The oft−heard "prestige" factor again clouded the Saturday ExCom session. Negative attitudes were further heightened because news arrived that an American U−2 plane had been shot down at 10:15 a.m. over Cuba, killing the pilot, Major Randolph Anderson, Jr. To ExCom members the U−2 downing, plus the two confusing Soviet letters, seemed to be further attempts at deceiving American leaders and delaying any new U.S. moves until all the Cuban missiles became operational. Apparently, no ExCom member knew enough about Soviet military defense procedures to understand that the decision to use the SAMs to shoot down the U−2 was probably a local command decision, not a Kremlin decision. As American analysts of Soviet policy realize, the fear of invasion was so endemic in Russian history that the Red Army's defense instructions were and are to respond against any territorial threat. Therefore, the odds were high — lacking direct knowledge of Moscow's intent — that because the SAMs in Cuba were installed and operated by Russian defense teams trained in defense procedures for the U.S.S.R., the SAM commanders reacted as trained.

Lacking expert advice, the ExCom and JFK immediately adopted the pedestrian judgement that the Kremlin's plot had thickened. Therefore, the ExCom expected the worst and sought to apply the contingency previously discussed regarding a proper U.S. response to the downing of a U−2 — that America would immediately retaliate by knocking out a

Russian SAM base in Cuba. Fortunately, this scenario included the proviso that the Air Force must check with President Kennedy before retaliating.

The ExCom "almost unanimously," according to Robert Kennedy, opted for an air strike against Cuba the next day. The president held back, however. He wanted more data on the U−2 incident and time to explore the Kremlin's final negotiating position. Fortunately, one ExCom member recalled that the Air Force might already be proceeding with its contingency plan to retaliate. Subsequently, a series of phone calls just managed to stop Air Force preparations for the air attack. The Air Force believed the retaliation order was automatic. This incident prompted some Air Force officers to suggest that Kennedy had folded and given in to the Kremlin.

When the ExCom reconvened on Saturday afternoon, the president had decided on one final attempt to avoid an American air strike and invasion. While Defense Department preparations would continue in anticipation of an all−out attack on Monday or Tuesday, the president prepared another note which offered Khrushchev a final chance to step away from possible war. Apparently at his brother's suggestion, the president agreed not to invade Cuba but ignored the request to remove the Turkish missiles. Khrushchev was warned that an immediate response was essential or the U.S. would take more serious action against Cuba. Within a day or two, the U.S. would act to remove the missile bases.[16]

In addition, Kennedy's Saturday letter to Khrushchev pledged that as soon as Russia stopped its missile construction and removed the Cuban missiles, the president would end the quarantine and negotiate a settlement along the lines of Khrushchev's October 26 letter. The Turkish base question was not mentioned, but Robert Kennedy was sent to tell Ambassador Dobrynin about American plans for the Turkish missiles.

On Saturday evening, Robert Kennedy carried a copy of the president's letter to Ambassador Dobrynin. He told the ambassador that the speed−up of Soviet missile activity in Cuba required immediate American action and that the U.S. would not wait long for the Soviet answer to his brother's message. The crisis must be settled or war would result. The U.S.S.R. must remove its offensive weapons from Cuba. Robert Kennedy orally pledged that the U.S. would not invade

Cuba, but stated that the president could not remove the Turkish missiles under duress. The Turkish missiles, he said, would soon be removed, but not under threat or without the approval of the NATO alliance. As Robert Kennedy left Dobrynin, he warned that Khrushchev's response to the president's letter must be made tomorrow.[17]

KHRUSHCHEV YIELDS, OCTOBER 28

At 9:00 a.m. on Sunday, October 28, Moscow radio broadcast the news that Khrushchev accepted Kennedy's deal to remove Russian missiles in exchange for a promise the U.S. would not invade Cuba. The official word reached Secretary of State Rusk at 11:00 a.m.
Khrushchev's message stated the Soviets agreed to stop work on the missile sites and to dismantle, crate and remove the weapons "which you described as offensive." The removal would be carried out under U.N. supervision. He informed the president that the missiles were intended to defend Cuba from an attack. Therefore, he added:

> I regard with respect and trust the statement you made in your message of 27 October 1962 that there would be no attack, no invasion of Cuba, and not only on the part of the United States, but also on the part of other nations of the Western Hemisphere, as you said in your same message. Then the motives which induced us to render assistance of such kind to Cuba disappear.

President Kennedy responded before receiving the official Soviet text. At noon, he released the U.S. acceptance statement to the press and to the Voice of America for transmission to Russia. Saying he welcomed Khrushchev's "statesmanlike decision to stop building bases in Cuba...," Kennedy added that the solution of the Cuban crisis permitted the governments of the world to give attention to ending the arms race and reducing tensions.[18]
With domestic politics evidently in mind, Kennedy did not refer to his Saturday offer to "give assurances against an invasion of Cuba." Although a deal had been made which saved Khrushchev's face, it had also reversed Kennedy's pre-crisis rhetoric against allowing communism to continue in Cuba. The president did not wish to emphasize, as Khrushchev had, the new American policy toward Cuba. The president's bellicose statements about "no compromise with communism in Cuba" had, henceforth, to cease or be qualified. His decision was

well worth the cost of a potential nuclear exchange. Nevertheless, right–wing critics of Kennedy such as Mario Lazo (Q–17), and Richard Nixon severely castigated the president. In 1964, Nixon wrote in *Reader's Digest* that Kennedy had "pulled defeat out of the jaws of victory."[19]

CASTRO OBJECTS TO THE WITHDRAWAL

Castro was angry at Khrushchev's decision to remove the Russian missile bases. Urged on by the Communist Chinese who hoped to gain influence at Russian expense, Castro refused to let either Secretary General U Thant or United Nations technicians enter Cuba to supervise the removal. Castro also argued with Anastas Mikoyan who Khrushchev sent to Havana to negotiate such an arrangement on November 2. While Castro refused to backdown and accept UN inspection, Mikoyan sympathetically stated that these were difficult days for the Cuban people and "the Soviet people are with Cuba body and soul."

Lacking UN assistance in Cuba and failing to gain permission for the Red Cross to act as the inspector, the United States verified the removal of the missiles by continuous U–2 surveillance of the Russian dismantling operations and a *modus operandi* with Moscow by which the Soviet naval captains removed tarpaulins which covered the missiles on their ships' decks so that U.S. naval observers could check the missiles as they sailed for home. The U.S. Navy finally reported on November 11, that 42 MRBMs had been counted on the decks of Russian ships. As stated by Deputy Defense Secretary Roswell Gilpatric, only MRBM missiles and warheads had reached Cuba before October 23.

On November 11, Gilpatric also acknowledged that the question of the IL–28 bombers had become a special problem. Castro claimed the bombers were a gift from the U.S.S.R. to the Cubans. After Kennedy insisted that the bombers must be removed as offensive weapons, Mikoyan persuaded Castro to allow them to be disassembled and removed.

On November 20, President Kennedy announced that Khrushchev agreed to remove the bombers from Cuba within 30 days and the U.S. was ending its naval quarantine. The IL–28's would be observed and counted as they left Cuba by the same method used to verify the withdrawal of the missiles. Because the Cuban government refused to cooperate with the United Nations, Kennedy said, the U.S. "has no choice but to pursue its own means of checking on military activities in Cuba." Finally, Kennedy asserted that the U.S. would not end its efforts to prevent Cuba from expanding its subversion in the Western Hemisphere. He noted, however, that "these policies are very different from any intent to launch a military invasion of the island."

The U.S. naval quarantine ended on November 20. The Soviet Union removed its 42 Soviet IL−28 bombers from Cuba between December 1 and 6, 1962. The Cuban missile crisis had ended.[20]

Both Kennedy and Khrushchev could claim a "victory." Khrushchev said he got what he wanted: an American pledge not to attack Cuba. Kennedy and his supporters argued that the president had been firm, that he withstood the Soviet effort to diminish U.S. nuclear superiority, and that the missiles were removed because of the president's special talents in handling the crisis situation.[21]

NOTES

1. Schlesinger, *Thousand Days*, 809−813; Frank Costigliola, "The Failed Design: Kennedy, DeGaulle, and the Struggle for Europe," *Diplomatic History* 8 (Summer 1984), 243−244.

2. R. Kennedy, "Thirteen Days", 53−55.

3. J.F. Kennedy, *Public Papers 1962*, 814−816. Later, scholars of international law suggested that "quarantine" was a term for the selective interdiction of ships carrying offensive weapons to a designated area. Don C. Piper, "The Cuban Missile Crisis and International Law," *World Affairs* 138 (Summer 1975), 27.

4. F. Parkinson, 136−150, 161−169.

5. R. Kennedy, *Thirteen Days*, 57−66; Dinerstein, *Making A Missile Crisis*, 217−233.

6. Allison, *Essence of Decision*, 127–132; Sorensen, *Kennedy*, 708–710; Admiral George W. Anderson, Jr., "The Navy and the Decision–Making Process in Diplomatic Crisis," *Proceedings of a U.S. Naval History Symposium* (Annapolis, MD: U.S. Naval Academy, 1973); Dan Caldwell, "A Research Note on the Quarantine of Cuba, October 1962," *International Studies Quarterly* 22 (Dec. 1978), 625–633.

7. R. Kennedy, *Thirteen Days*, 67–72, Anderson, "The Navy and Decision–Making," 217–220.

8. Sorensen, *Kennedy*, 821–822.

9. Adlai Stevenson, *Papers of Adlai Stevenson*, 8 vols., edited by Walter Johnson (Boston: Little, Brown, 1972–1979), Vol. III. 331–332.

10. *Ibid.*, 220–221; R. Kennedy, *Thirteen Days*, 135–138; Hilsman, *To Move A Nation*, 217–220. Hilsman disclosed the Fomin–Scali incident in an article: "The Cuban Crisis: How Close We Were to War," *Look* 28 (Aug. 25, 1962), 17–21.

11. John Scherer, "Reinterpreting Soviet Behavior During the Cuban Missile Crisis," *World Affairs* 144 (Fall 1981), 110–125.

12. Hilsman, *To Move A Nation*, 219.

13. R. Kennedy, *Thirteen Days*, 135–138; Allison, *Essence of Decision*, 220–221. 14. Scherer, "Reinterpreting Soviet Behavior," 116–119.

15. Barton Bernstein, "The Cuban Missile Crisis: Trading the Jupiters in Turkey?" *Political Science Quarterly* 95 (Spring 1980), 97–125; George Harris, *Troubled Alliance: Turkish–American Problems in Historical Perspective 1945–1971* (Washington, DC: Brookings Institution, 1972), 85–95. The ExCom recording of the October 16 session indicates President Kennedy asked how many missiles were in Turkey and was told there were fifteen. *ExCom Sess. Oct. 16*, first session, 14.

16. Bernstein, "Trading the Jupiters," 117–123; R. Kennedy, *Thirteen Days*, 93–106; Allison, *Essence of Decision*, 223–230; Donald L. Hafner, "Bureaucratic Politics and Those Frigging Missiles : JFK, Cuba and U.S. Missiles in Turkey," *Orbis* 21 (Summer 1977), 307–333.

17. R. Kennedy, *Thirteen Days*, 107–110; Arthur Schlesinger, Jr., *Robert F. Kennedy and His Times* (Boston: Houghton Mifflin, 1978), 543–547.

18. The Kennedy–Khrushchev message may be found in *U.S. Department of State Bulletin* 69 (Nov. 19, 1973), 640–655.

19. Richard Nixon, "Cuba, Castro, and John F. Kennedy," *Reader's Digest* 85 (Nov. 1964), 283–300.

20. Data on post–crisis activity to November 20, 1962 is listed in Facts–on–File, *Cuba, The U.S. and Russia*, 78–89.

21. Among Kennedy's advisors, individuals held divergent views on tactics. They shared, however, an essential Cold War frame of reference, assuming the U.S. had to act forcefully in foreign relations. David Halberstam describes the two factions in the Democratic Party: hard–line cold warriors led by Dean Acheson and a "soft–line" group led by Eleanor Roosevelt and Stevenson which sought to end the arms race and encourage economic–social reform in the Third World as the main issue, relegating the Soviet Cold War relations to lesser priority. Kennedy had straddled the fence between the two groups but became a real cold warrior as Eleanor Roosevelt suspected during 1961. Thus, by 1962, Chester Bowles had been removed as Undersecretary of State, W. Averell Harriman headed the Far East Division but was not on the ExCom. Stevenson's treatment during and after the crisis indicates the consequences for someone who openly dissented from Kennedy's inner circle. Halberstam, *Best and Brightest*, 18–34, 51–53, 88–89; and Richard Walton, *Cold War and Counterrevolution*, 4–6. On Stevenson, see Bernstein, "Trading Jupiters," 104–107.

V

Summary

Following Khrushchev's acceptance of Kennedy's proposal, the one remaining phase of the crisis was verification of the missiles removal. Even before the removal was complete on November 20, however, both Khrushchev and Kennedy had formulated victory statements. Khrushchev claimed he had won because Kennedy had pledged not to invade Cuba thereby fulfilling the alleged communist goal. Kennedy's spokesmen persuaded most Americans that the president had won because Khrushchev backed down in the face of Kennedy's firmness and American military superiority. Neither leaders' rationalizations have stood the test of post−crisis analysis.

KENNEDY AND KHRUSHCHEV CLAIM VICTORY

The U.S. claim of military superiority as a critical factor in the withdrawal decision was a superficial argument which did not represent the Kremlin's reasons for withdrawing. The Russian leaders had understood the existence of U.S. military superiority *before* they sent the missiles to Cuba. The Presidium had accepted Khrushchev's gamble in an attempt to increase their deterrent capacity vis−a−vis the existing U.S. superiority. As soon as Kennedy announced the naval quarantine and threatened to escalate his military response, Moscow simply sought to salvage its prestige in an agreement to withdraw. Consequently, Moscow asked on October 26 and 27, that the U.S. promise not to invade Cuba and that it remove the Turkish missiles to offset the sting of withdrawing its missiles from Cuba.[1]

Nor was Kennedy's firmness a key factor in the Soviet decision to withdraw their missiles. A strong private diplomatic show of determination, such as Bohlen suggested on October 18, might have yielded similar results. As Bernstein, Etzioni (M−23), and Nathan (M−28) demonstrate, Kennedy was consciously flexible in establishing the blockade and dealing with the Soviet leaders. Although he did not directly pledge to remove the Turkish missiles, Robert Kennedy's statement to Ambassador Dobrynin implied that the Jupiter missiles would not remain in Turkey much longer. Thus, while Kennedy hedged on the Turkish statement, the Soviets agreed to withdraw on the basis of JFK's promise not to invade Cuba.

If Kennedy's apologists desired to sharpen their leader's image as firm and his military expenditures as necessary, Khrushchev's claim to have won a round as the protector of a Third World nation was equally self-serving. Although admitting that Kennedy's pledge saved face for Khrushchev, later studies deny this rationalization as being Khrushchev's reason for the missile gamble. Graham Allison's text and footnotes offer the strongest possible case for Khrushchev's claim. Yet, Allison concludes that the Soviets could have deterred an American attack on Cuba without basing MRBMs and IRBMs on that island. The conventional equipment Moscow had sent to Cuba was adequate to deter any discreet U.S. effort to intervene; thus, a major U.S. attack would be necessary to depose Castro. If deterrence of a Cuban attack had been the Soviet rationale, a contingent of Russian troops could have played the same role that American troops played in West Berlin. As Allison asserts, "it is difficult to conceive of a Soviet deployment of weapons less suited to the purpose of Cuban defense than the one the Soviets made." At best, the defense of Cuba had been a subsidiary cause of Khrushchev's gamble.[2]

SOVIET MISCALCULATIONS

Post-crisis analysis showed that while Khrushchev sought major strategic advantages over the United States, the Kremlin had miscalculated. As George and Smoke indicate, the Soviet Presidium viewed the decision to place the missiles in Cuba as a low-risk venture with possible high returns in terms of strategic gains in the nuclear weapons balance and, possibly, in relation to the Berlin issue or the Turkish missile bases. However, what began as a low-risk operation had suddenly become a high-risk situation by October 23.

The Soviets had underestimated both the speed with which U.S. intelligence would locate the missiles and the quickness with which Kennedy introduced a military-type response. The Soviets had hoped that rapid base construction and political deception would enable them to have the missile sites operational by November 15 at which time

Khrushchev would publicize the Soviet's installations as an accomplished fact during the November United Nations meeting. Khrushchev could then mobilize Third World backing in the UN to prevent the U.S. from attacking the missile sites in Cuba or from finding any satisfactory diplomatic method of removing them. In the Kremlin's scenario, the American leaders would have to accept nuclear parity with the Soviets and would have to treat Soviet interests and proposals more equitably.

But the Soviet scenario was flawed. The U.S. discovery of the missile construction on October 14 and Kennedy's subsequent quarantine of Soviet shipments to Cuba forced the Kremlin leaders to confront a bitter dilemma: should they challenge the blockade and risk a destructive nuclear war or should they withdraw the missiles and seek some means to salvage their prestige.

From the studies of Allison, Herbert Dinerstein, and John Scherer, a picture emerges of the Kremlin's "hawks" and "doves" debating the proper course of action. Although Scherer's recent analysis of the October 26–27 letters concludes Khrushchev was a "hawk" and other Presidium members were "doves," most previous analysts assumed Khrushchev was a "dove." Whichever version may be correct, available data from Soviet sources indicates that from October 23 to 27 Soviet leaders sought some face-saving concessions which would permit them to comply with Kennedy's requirement that they remove their missiles. Thus, the President's October 27 indication that he would pledge not to attack Cuba, as well as Robert Kennedy's assurances to Dobrynin that the Jupiter missiles in Turkey would be removed in the near future, gave Khrushchev two "justifications" for withdrawing from the unacceptable high risk confrontation.[3]

Analysis indicates that the Soviet Union's miscalculations were also due partly to America's inconsistent statements and action. For example, the U.S. asserted that its missiles in Turkey and other NATO countries were defensive and emphasized that these weapons were controlled by Americans not Europeans. When, however, the Soviet Union claimed its missiles in Cuba were defensive and several times asserted that Soviet officers, not Cubans, controlled the missiles, the U.S. insisted the Soviet missiles were "offensive." Because deterrence analysis is designed to deter by avoiding miscalculations of intention, such misperceptions are significant. For both superpowers, any nuclear missile within the range of its home territory was clearly perceived as offensive, while any missile outside the range of its homeland might be construed as defensive. Yet, both superpowers have been reluctant to formally accept this definition.[4]

Finally, the Soviet leaders misjudged American responses because they did not understand Kennedy's domestic political situation in 1962 — a situation American politicians routinely face but Soviet politicians do not — that is, the need to convey different images to different constituencies under varying circumstances. JFK's moderate September response to the SAM missiles was not simply a signal to Moscow; it was also an effort to counteract the Republican Party's attempt to make Cuba a political issue in the congressional elections. Subsequently, the mild September response necessitated Kennedy's strong reaction in October when the Republican predications seemed to be valid. Challenging an American president is more dangerous during an election year because U.S. election dates are immovable and politicians fear any last-minute changes in public perceptions may defeat them.

Apparently, some Soviet leaders realized their miscalculations on October 23. The nervous and "shaken" moods of Dobrynin, Zorin, and Gromyko which reporters detected between October 23 and 28, were probably honest reactions to their unfulfilled expectations. Kennedy's publicly proclaimed naval quarantine, his threat of further military action, and his immediate diplomatic offensive before the November elections had not been anticipated by the Soviets. On October 23, however, Khrushchev realized that the blockade was an "initial" U.S. military response which could, and probably would, be expanded, depending on whether Russia removed its missiles from Cuba.[5]

Herbert Dinerstein's thematic analysis of the October 23 Soviet government statement and of editorial comments in the Russian Army's *Red Star*, compared with the Kremlin's official papers, *Pravda* and *Izvestia*, demonstrates that the Soviet leadership immediately altered the emphasis of its Cuban policy. While earlier statements suggested the U.S.S.R. would defend Castro even at the risk of a Soviet-American war, the October 23 Russian statements and reports implied the Soviet Union never intended to use nuclear weapons in defending Cuba. Although the "hawkish" *Red Star* military paper said the Soviet Union need not negotiate, *Pravda*, a government organ, appealed to the United Nations to stop America's illegal acts and called on "all peace-loving" peoples to defend Cuba. Similarly, the Soviet government statement suggested that the UN had a role in the crisis and asserted the U.S.S.R. would not unleash its military forces unless aggression had been committed by the United States. Thus, Russian rhetoric changed on October 23 from statements about defending Cuba with Soviet rockets to proposals urging the U.N. and "peace—loving peoples" to defend Cuba.[6]

In addition to the October 23 statements, the Soviet failure to challenge the blockade on October 24 should have been a strong message to President Kennedy that the Soviets intended to withdraw their missiles given the proper conditions. The CIA reported that there were no Soviet preparations for war after October 23, and Averell Harriman saw conciliatory signals in Khrushchev's meeting with William Knox and Jerome Hines on October 23. Sorensen informed Kennedy about Harriman's views. If the president phoned Harriman, as Sorensen assumes, there was, however, no evidence that Kennedy acted on October 25 or 26 in conjunction with Harriman's advice.

THE OCTOBER 26 AND 27 LETTERS

The White House seemed to expect the worst from October 24 to 26 and "Black Saturday" appeared to bring the worst. The receipt of two conflicting notes from Khrushchev on October 26 and 27, together with the shooting down of the U−2, brought the ExCom to the verge of executing an unannounced air strike against Cuba.

Since 1962, American analysts have had difficulty explaining the October 26 and 27 letters from Moscow. As Allison indicates, most studies follow the White House opinion in associating the Scali−Fomin exchange with the Khrushchev's Friday night letter, because the letter seemed to correlate with the Fomin offer of a deal involving a no−invasion pledge in exchange for the missiles' removal. This interpretation makes Khrushchev a "dove" seeking a minimal demand while the October 27 letter casts the Presidium as "hawks" who demanded the removal of Turkish missiles as well as the no−invasion pledge.

In 1981, John Scherer challenged this thesis. Using the original Russian language texts of Khrushchev's letters and other documents released between 1973 and 1981, Scherer contends that Fomin's talk with Scali regarding a U.S. pledge not to attack Cuba represented the soft−line Presidium approach to salvaging some Soviet prestige while Khrushchev's two letters expressed his hard−line, impulsive attempt to demand more from Kennedy. As noted previously, Scherer contends that Khrushchev offered no concessions in the critical paragraph of his

October 26 letter but tried to force Kennedy to make concessions which might be followed by Castro's demobilization. The October 27 letter continued Khrushchev's hard–line approach by requesting the pledge not to invade Cuba as well as a promise to remove the Jupiter missiles from Turkey.

According to Scherer's interpretation, moderates in the Presidium, such as M.A. Suslov, Alexei N. Kosygin and Leonoid Brezhnev, wanted Khrushchev to relax his hard–line toward the Cuban missiles. On Saturday, October 27, Kennedy's so–called "Trollope ploy" unknowingly selected the Presidium's request for the promise not to invade Cuba and ignored Khrushchev's request to remove the Turkish bases. Scherer's explanation mitigates the ExCom's confusion during its Saturday meeting after Khrushchev's second letter arrived. There was perhaps no American in Washington on October 27 who could have discerned the sources of Fomin's message as differing from that of Khrushchev's two letters. For students of Soviet behavior, however, Scherer's conjecture makes the point that if an unexpected Soviet move is made, such as the Fomin–Scali contact, American decision makers should study it carefully for a possible signal of dissent within the Soviet government.[7]

Both the Fomin–Scali exchange and Khrushchev's second letter asked Kennedy to agree not to invade Cuba, a proposal designed to preserve Moscow's leadership among the Third World socialists against China's attempt to dislodge Moscow. Mao Tse–tung watched the Cuban crisis carefully, not only to denounce America's imperialists but to discover some method of demonstrating Moscow's incompetence in promoting socialism. Khrushchev's gamble in Cuba gave Peking an opportunity to replace Moscow as the leader of the Third World, but Kennedy's pledge not to invade Cuba saved Khrushchev's position of favor among the former colonial nations.

One other point has been made about the impact of the Khrushchev letters. Because the ExCom was confused when the second letter arrived, its members misinterpreted the shooting down of the U–2 over Cuba as the Kremlin's attempt to prolong the Cuban crisis. Most post–crisis analysts disagree with the ExCom assessment, pointing out that the Soviet Union's military organizational methods decentralized command decisions, particularly in decisions regarding the defense of Soviet territory and materials. Moreover, like most bureaucracies, the Soviet organization does not function as harmoniously as many Americans presume. As studies by Tatu, Kolkowicz, and Allison agree,

Soviet "hawks" and "doves" exist and there is persisting friction between high-ranking leaders in the Kremlin.

Although American analysts lack much documentation about Soviet organizational behavior, available evidence indicates Soviet SAM commmanders in Cuba acted according to their normal orders to use the SAMs as soon as they became operational. When the crisis began on October 23, no one in Moscow's command structure abrogated the earlier orders to the SAM officials in Cuba. Although some U.S. analysts contend that "hawks" in Moscow ordered the SAM attack to prevent Khrushchev from removing the missiles, the evidence for this interpretation appears less credible than the bureaucratic orders-in-being interpretation. American accounts of Saturday, October 27, indicate the White House almost forgot to check if the U.S. Air Force realized it should *not* retaliate without Kennedy's approval. Someone in the ExCom remembered to check with the Air Force, a recollection which, regarding the SAMs, the Moscow leaders may have overlooked as they struggled to back away from their miscalculation of Kennedy's policy toward Cuba.

Certainly, post-crisis studies find no evidence for the ExCom views that in October, Khrushchev was continuing to plan war against the United States. Fortunately, President Kennedy seems to have realized this; perhaps, because as the person with final responsibility for decisions on war and peace, he wanted to be certain that all peaceful avenues had been tried before deciding for war. Thus, on Saturday, October 27, JFK paused before accepting the ExCom recommendation to attack Cuba. According to Robert Kennedy, the president said, "It isn't the first step that concerns me, but both sides escalating to the fourth and fifth step — and we don't go to the sixth because there is no one around to do so." Soon after, Kennedy informed the Soviet leaders he would accept the October 26 Russian offer and the crisis ended.

NOTES

1. Allison, *Essence of Decision*, 62-66; Barton J. Bernstein, "The Week We Almost Went To War," 13-21; Amitai Etzioni, "The Kennedy Experiment," *Western Political Quarterly* 20 (June 1967), 361-380.

2. For Khrushchev's version, see *Khrushchev Remembers* (Boston: Little, Brown, 1970), 488–505; and *The Last Testament* (Boston: Little, Brown, 1974), 509–514; Allison, *Essence of Decision*, 48–50.

3. Allison, *Essence of Decision*, 64–66, 140, 218–224; Scherer, "Reinterpreting Soviet Behavior," 111–115.

4. During NATO discussions on deployment of the U.S. missiles in Europe, most NATO members feared the decision would antagonize Moscow and refused the weapons. The U.S. believed they were defensive missiles because Washington assumed the Western powers would not strike first. Armacost, *Politics of Weapons Innovation*, 175–211. Americans generally believed their forces in Europe were "defensive;" the Russians saw them as "offensive." As noted above (Chap. 3, note 3), Kennedy did not adequately answer a reporter's question on September 13, 1962, regarding the definition of "offensive" and "defensive."

5. Allison, *Essence of Decision*, 134–135; George and Smoke, *Deterrence in American Foreign Policy*, 463–466.

6. Dinerstein, *Making of Missile Crisis*, 217–222.

7. Scherer, "Reinterpreting Soviet Behavior," 110–121.

VI

References

There are several general studies which summarize the basic information about the events of the Cuban missile crisis. The best such introduction is Divine's volume (A−5) which, while somewhat dated, provides essential data on the October events and several essays giving divergent contemporary interpretations of the crisis. For students desiring an analytical approach to the crisis, Allison's book (A−2) is an excellent place to begin.

Other satisfactory introductions to the crisis are those written by Abel (A−1), who had close friends on Kennedy's staff, and Detzer (A−4). An article by Robert A. Hurwitch (A−15) gives a brief summation of the crisis, while a 1963 State Department publication (A−9) has a chronology of events in U.S.−Cuban relations from 1957 to 1963. Anyone desiring to read a Soviet version of the crisis should review the volume by Gromyko (A−7).

ANALYTICAL AND HISTORICAL STUDIES

The historiography of the Cuban missile crisis may, at present, be divided into two parts: the contemporary accounts published before 1970, and the more analytical accounts which appeared in print after 1971. While many of the early accounts by observers, pundits, and participants in the crisis provided the essential information for later analysis, the studies published after Allison's *Essence of Decision* (1971) are characterized by the more objective use of documents, primary source material, and often the application of theoretical models similar to or differing with Allison's.

Allison described three analytical models: the classical or rational actor, the organizational process, and the governmental−bureaucratic−political model. The classical model was the traditional method used by scholars to explain rational considerations and choices made by a nation or its leaders. The organizational model emphasized the standard operating procedures used by government agencies which circumscribed the rational actor's role in decisions. The governmental politics model investigated how groups, which shared power within the government, played bargaining games which arrived at a collegially determined course of action. Allison acknowledged the experimental nature of his second and third models but suggested the importance of these two decision structures in impinging on the classical model. As Allison noted, the interaction of these models could further enlighten understanding of crisis—management, deterrent policy in action, and classical decision making studies. After 1971, scholars would challenge, alter, or clarify such models but could not either implicitly or explicitly ignore them.

Historical study of the 1962 crisis has evolved a pattern somewhat similar to the pre— and post—Allison interpretations. During most of the decade immediately following the Cuban crisis, the best known studies focused on President Kennedy's "finest hour" as being his strong stance and management of the crisis from October 22 to 28, 1962.

During the early 1970's, revisionist historians of the Kennedy years sought to prick holes in the Kennedy legend. Although some writers continued to defend Kennedy's policies, more writers used documents which gradually became available in order to reject the previous "Camelot" version of the Kennedy years. These critical assessments of President Kennedy influenced the study of his 1000 days in office, but focused particularly on the "finest hour" interpretation of Kennedy during the October crisis.

In brief, students using reference materials on the missile crisis may often, but not always, assume that books and articles published before 1969 will interpret the Cuban crisis more favorably toward Kennedy than those written after 1970.

A. *General Surveys*

In addition to the studies mentioned previously as the best introductory accounts, notable general books on the Cuban crisis are those written by Beggs (A−3), Pachter (A−8), and Weintal and Bartlett (A−10). Although it is unusually weak on the events preceding October 1962, the Facts on File volume (A−6) is a useful chronology based on news headlines relating to Cuban—American relations from 1959 to 1962.

Although Allison's book is the best general study with which to analyze the 1962 crisis, he also explained his categories in a 1969 essay (A−11). Other essays which provide general accounts of the 1962 crisis include those written by Bernstein (A−12), Draper (A−13), McDonough (A−16), Rodman (S−15), and Statsenko (A−17). In addition to his book, Soviet historian Gromyko (A−14) wrote an essay to summarize his belief that the crisis was a U.S. plot to overthrow Castro.

(Books)

A−1 Abel, Elie. *The Missile Crisis*. New York: Praeger, 1966.

A−2 Allison, Graham T. *Essence of Decision: Explaining the Cuban Missile Crisis*. Boston: Little, Brown, 1971.

A−3 Beggs, Robert. *The Cuban Missile Crisis*. London: Longman, 1971.

A−4 Detzer, David. *The Brink: Cuban Missile Crisis, 1962*. New York: Crowell, 1979.

A−5 Divine, Robert A., ed. *The Cuban Missile Crisis: The Continuing Debate*. Chicago: Quadrangle, 1971.

A−6 Facts on File. *Cuba, The United States, and Russia, 1960−1963*. New York: Facts on File, 1964.

A−7 Gromyko, Anatolii Andreievich. *Through Russian Eyes: President Kennedy's 1036 Days*. Trans. by Philip A. Garon. Washington, DC: International Library, 1973.

A−8 Pachter, Henry. *Collison Course: The Cuban Missile Crisis and Coexistence*. New York: Praeger, 1963.

A−9 U.S. Department of State. *Events in United States−Cuban Relations, A Chronology, 1957−1963*. Washington, DC: G.P.O., 1963.

A—10 Weintal, Edward and Charles Bartlett. *Facing the Brink.* New York: Scribner's, 1967.

(Essays)

A—11 Allison, Graham T., "Conceptual Models and the Cuban Crisis." *American Political Science Reveiw* 63 (September 1969), 689—718. Also published as "Conceptual Models and the Cuban Missile Crisis: National Policy, Organization Process and Bureaucratic Politics". Santa Monica, CA: Rand Corp., 1968.

A—12 Bernstein, Barton J. "The Week We Almost Went to War." *Bulletin of the Atomic Scientists* 32 (Feb. 1976), 13—21.

A—13 Draper, Theodore. "Castro and Communism: A Detailed Account of the Background and Consequences of the Missile Crisis in Cuba." *Reporter* 28 (Jan. 17, 1963), 35—48.

A—14 Gromyko, Anatolii. "The Caribbean Crisis: The U.S. Government's Preparation of the Crisis and the Efforts of the U.S.S.R. to Eliminate the Crisis." *Soviet Law and Government* 11 (Summer 1972), 3—53.

A—15 Hurwitch, Robert A. "The Cuban Missile Crisis." *Foreign Service Journal* 48:7 (1971), 17—20.

A—16 McDonough, Joseph A. "Crisis Diplomacy: Cuba 1962." *Naval War College Review* 19 (Summer 1966), 1—35.

A—17 Statsenko, Igor. "Sobre Algunos Aspectos Politico—Militares de la Crisis del Caribe." ["Political—Military Aspects of the Caribbean Crisis"], *Amerika Latina* (U.S.S.R.) 3 (1978), 140—150.

B. *Some Contemporary Assessments*

During the two years following the October 1962 crisis, commentary about the events divided along usual political lines: many strongly favored Kennedy's action from October 22 to 28 as "his finest hour";

some to the left of center criticized the president for not avoiding the military confrontation; others to the right of center complained because he did not use the opportunity to eliminate communism in Cuba. Based entirely on the public record and "leaks" from government agencies, these three positions predominated until the 1970's.

In addition to media reports, which largely praised Kennedy immediately after the crisis, the ground rules for the president's favorable assessment were laid by a journalist, Alsop (B−1), who used Bartlett's close relationship with the White House to gain details of Kennedy's "victory" over Khrushchev. In December 1962, Alsop also published an article (B−2) on Kennedy's "new strategy" to avoid nuclear war, an effort designed to calm the U.S. public's fears of a nuclear holocaust. The first book−size account which favored the president's role was published in 1963 by a British journalist, Pachter (A−8). Later, journalist Abel (A−1) used his Washington sources to construct a lengthy pro−Kennedy version of the crisis.

Critical commentaries on the U.S. handling of the crisis also appeared during these early years. In this category may be included essays by Ascoli (B−3), Crane (B−7), Draper (A−13), Hilsman (M−50), Kissinger (B−14), Lippman (B−15), Kahan and Lang (B−13), Mackintosh (B−16), Morgenthau (B−17), and Neustadt (B−18). Steele (M−44) added information on Adlai Stevenson which qualified Alsop's article regarding the Ambassador's role.

Because nuclear war seemed imminent on October 27, many left−wing critics argued that Kennedy's failure to use diplomacy had created an unnecessary crisis by exaggerating the danger of Cuban missiles. Dewart's (B−9) description of the events leading to the crisis viewed the president as having conspired to challenge Khrushchev. Writers such as Chase (B−6), and Bernstein and Hagen (B−4) emphasized the low risk of the Cuban missiles which contrasted with Kennedy's rhetoric on and after October 22. In separate articles, both Bernstein (B−5) and Hagen (B−10) indicated that, as Secretary of Defense McNamara had commented to the ExCom during the crisis, intermediate range missiles in Cuba did not change the nuclear balance. Commentators who criticized the President for not using diplomacy and for raising tensions with the Soviets because of the renewed nuclear testing in 1962, included Jenkins (B−11), Pomerance (B−20), Rabinowich (B−21) and Stone (B−22 and B−23).

Writers on the right−wing were equally critical of Kennedy for his "softness" during the October crisis. By January 1963, Johnson's (B−

12) and Lowenthal's (Q−18) articles led the way by describing Kennedy's October response to the communists as inadequate. Shortly after, Daniel and Hubbell (B−8) wrote a detailed critical account which appeared in condensed form in the March 1963 *Reader's Digest*. Other notable right−wing criticisms of Kennedy appeared in articles by Toledano (B−24) and Varney (B−25) and in a book by Lazo (Q−17). Richard Nixon (B−19) thought Kennedy was right to call Khrushchev's bluff, but had failed to follow through in a tough fashion.

Generally, an excellent sampling of the divergent early views on the missile crisis may be found in Divine's (A−5) volume. Scholars desiring a detailed bibliography of material published between 1962 and 1966 should consult the listing in Gillingham (T−7).

B−1   Alsop, Stewart and Charles Bartlett. "In Time of Crisis." *Saturday Evening Post* 235 (Dec. 8, 1962), 16−20.

B−2   Alsop, Stewart. "Our New Strategy: The Alternative to Total War." *Saturday Evening Post* 235 (Dec. 1, 1962), 13−18.

B−3   Ascoli, Max. "Escalation from the Bay of Pigs." *Reporter* 27 (Nov. 8, 1962), 24−25.

B−4   Bernstein, Barton and Roger Hagen. "Military Value of Missiles in Cuba." *Bulletin of the Atomic Scientists* 19 (Feb. 1963), 8−13.

B−5   Bernstein, Barton J. "Their Finest Hour?" *Correspondent* 32 (Aug. 1964), 119−121.

B−6   Chase, Stuart. "Political Missiles in Cuba." *War/Peace Report* 3 (Feb. 1963), 9−10.

B−7   Crane, Robert D. "The Cuban Crisis: A Strategic Analysis of American and Soviet Policy." *Orbis* 6 (Winter 1965), 528−563.

B−8   Daniel, James and John G. Hubbell. *Strike in the West*. New York: Holt, Rinehart & Winston, 1963.

B–9 Dewart, Leslie. "The Cuban Crisis Revisited." *Studies on the Left* 5 (Spring 1965), 15–40.

B–10 Hagen, Roger. "Triumph or Tragedy?" *Dissent* 10 (Winter 1963), 13–26.

B–11 Jenkins, Ray. "How Close Did We Come to War Over Cuba?" *War/Peace Report* 3 (Dec. 1963), 3–6.

B–12 Johnson, Major General Max. S. (ret.) "Who Really Gained in Cuba Showdown?" *U.S. News and World Report* 53 (Nov. 12, 1962), 45.

B–13 Kahan, Jerome H. and Anne K. Lang. "The Cuban Missile Crisis: A Study of its Strategic Context." *Political Science Quarterly* 87 (Dec. 1972), 564–590.

B–14 Kissinger, Henry. "Reflections on Cuba." *Reporter* 27 (Nov. 22, 1962), 21–24.

B–15 Lippman, Walter. "Cuba and the Nuclear Risk." *Atlantic* 211 (Feb. 1963), 55–58.

B–16 Mackintosh, J. Malcolm. "Soviet Motives in Cuba." *Survival* 5 (Jan.–Feb., 1963), 16–18.

B–17 Morgenthau, Hans J. "Cuba: The Wake of Isolation." *Commentary* 34 (Nov. 1962), 427–430.

B–18 Neustadt, Richard. "Kennedy and the Presidency: A Premature Appraisal." *Political Science Quarterly* 79 (Sept. 1964), 321–334.

B–19 Nixon, Richard. "Cuba, Castro and John F. Kennedy." *Reader's Digest* 85 (Nov. 1964), 283–300.

B-20 Pomerance, Josephine W. "The Cuban Missile Crisis and the Test Ban Negotiations." *Journal of Conflict Resolution* 7:3 (1963), 553-559.

B-21 Rabinowich, Eugene. "After Cuba: Two Lessons." *Bulletin of the Atomic Scientists* 19 (Feb. 1963), 2-8.

B-22 Stone, I. F. "The Brink." *New York Review of Books* 6 (Apr. 14, 1966), 12-16.

B-23 Stone, I. F. "Fresh Light on the Mystery of the Missiles." *I. F. Stone Weekly* 11 (Jan. 14, 1963), 6.

B-24 Toledano, R. "Cuba Story: Wraps Off." *National Review* 14 (Aug. 9, 1963), 288-289.

B-25 Varney, Harold L. *Cuba: The Truth--We Shout Victory, But Khrushchev Still Has Cuba.* New York: Committee on Pan-American Policy, 1963.

C. *Domestic American Politics*

During the 1960 presidential campaign, John F. Kennedy and the Democrats strongly criticized the Eisenhower Administration policies toward Cuba. The developments in Cuban-American relations during the 1950's have been described in doctoral dissertations by Bonachea (Q-3) and Tierney (Q-14). Three Americans who were closely connected with U.S. policy in Cuba during the late 1950's have written personal accounts of their experience--Berle (C-2), Smith (C-6), and Bonsal (C-3). Smith, who was Eisenhower's Ambassador to Cuba during Batista's last years, is particularly critical of the State Department's "liberal" policies as tending to favor Castro.

Beck (C-1) deals with Kennedy's lack of specific knowledge about Eisenhower's initial training of Cuban exiles for the liberation of their homeland. During the campaign, the third of the celebrated Nixon-Kennedy debates included exchanges on Cuba. The debate texts may be found in Kraus' edition of The Great Debates (C-4). During its 1960 Executive Sessions, the Senate Foreign Relations Committee

(Q−26) had several briefings on the Cuban situation. White (C−7) became famous for his sympathetic account of Kennedy's 1960 campaign. Tom Wicker (C−8) examines how Cuba became a campaign issue by October 1962.

C−1 Beck, Kent M. "Necessary Lies, Hidden Truths: Cuba in the 1960 Campaign." *Diplomatic History* 8 (Winter 1984), 37−59.

C−2 Berle, Adolf A., Jr., "The Cuban Crisis, Failure of American Foreign Policy." *Foreign Affairs* 39 (Oct. 1960), 40−55.

C−3 Bonsal, Philip W. "Cuba, Castro and the United States." *Foreign Affairs* 45 (Jan. 1967), 260−276.

C−4 Kraus, Sidney. *The Great Debates (1960)*. Glouchester, MA: Peter Smith, 1968.

C−5 "Senator John F. Kennedy on the Cuban Situation: The Presidential Campaign of 1960." *Inter−American Economics Affairs* 15 (Winter 1961), 5−6.

C−6 Smith, Earl E. T. *The Fourth Floor*. New York: Random House, 1962.

C−7 White, Theodore. *The Making of the President, 1960*. New York: New American Library, 1967.

C−8 Wicker, Tom. "Cuba Emerging as Issue at the Polls." *New York Times International Edition* (Oct. 2, 1962), 4.

D. *"Missile Gap" Issue*

In addition to attacking the Republican's Cuban policy, the Kennedy−Johnson ticket of 1960 also criticized the Eisenhower Administration for weakness in allowing the alleged "missile−gap" to develop which, they said, would give the Soviet Union a nuclear ICBM edge during the 1960's. Aliano (D-1) describes the political controversy surrounding the missile-gap between 1957 and 1961. Bottome (D-3) and Licklider (D-6) survey the technical aspects of the missile-gap issue including the U.S. decision to delay constructing liquid-fuel ICBM's because solid-fuel ones would be better weapons, a decision which Moscow also made. Ball (D-2) explains how the Kennedy Administration continued its program to rapidly build 1000 Minuteman ICBM's even after they learned that the missile-gap charge was a myth. An interesting article by Murphy (D-7) argues that Khrushchev had "bamboozled" the U.S. with his rocket-rattling and believed in 1962 he could again bluff the Americans and regain strategic ground in Cuba.

Four authors relate the missile-gap theory to the broader context of the nuclear dispute. Boyer (S-4) describes the fear of the 1950's. York (D-9), a nuclear physicist who was an advisor to both the Eisenhower and Kennedy administrations, provides an insider's view of the developments following the Sputnik launching in 1957. Dick (D-4) and Schell (D-8) both explore the long-term consequences of the missile-gap dispute. Gray (D-5) claims that Kennedy's 1961 announcements of American nuclear superiority (there was no missile gap) induced Khrushchev to place missiles in Cuba in 1962.

D-1 Aliano, Richard A. *American Defense Policy from Eisenhower to Kennedy: The Politics of ChangingMilitary Requirements, 1957-1961.* Athens: Ohio University Press, 1975.

D-2 Ball, Desmond. *Politics and Force Levels: The Strategic Missile Program of the Kennedy Administration.* Berkeley: University of California Press, 1981.

D-3 Bottome, Edgar M. *The Missile Gap.* Cranbury, NJ: Fairleigh Dickinson University Press, 1970.

D-4 Dick, James C. "The Strategic Arms Race, 1957-1961: Who Opened a Missile Gap?" *Journal of Politics* 34 (Nov. 1972), 1062-1110.

D-5 Gray, Colin S. "Gap Prediction and America's Defense: Arms Race Behavior in the Eisenhower Years." *Orbis* 16 (Spring 1972), 257-74.

D-6 Licklider, Roy E. "The Missile Gap Controversy." *Political Science Quarterly* 85 (Dec. 1970), 600-615.

D-7 Murphy, Charles S. V. "Khrushchev's Paper Bear." *Fortune* 70 (Dec. 1964), 115, 224-230.

D-8 Schell, Jonathan. *The Time of Illusion.* New York: Knopf, 1976.

D-9 York, Herbert F. *Race to Oblivion: A Participant's View of the Arms Race.* New York: Simon & Schuster, 1970.

E. *Intelligence Operations: CIA and U-2*

Immediately after the crisis ended, critics complained that U.S. intelligence had failed to accurately report Soviet activity in Cuba. Burnham (E-2) described intelligence weakness in a *National Review* article. As a result of such complaints, the Defense Department (E-3 and E-12) conducted a special briefing on intelligence on February 6, 1962. In addition, the Senate Armed Services Committee (E-11) investigated the U-2 data and Amon Katz (E-5) prepared a Rand Corporation study. Hilsman (M-54), the head of the State Department's Bureau of Intelligence and Research, gave extensive time to the issue in his memoirs and in an exchange of views with Ronald Steel (M-55). Krock's memoirs (E-7) include data on CIA Director McCone's situation in 1962. Before scholars gained access to CIA reports (L-8) in the fall of 1982, Knorr (E-6) had written the best summary of intelligence estimates on Cuba. Spokesmen such as Laird (E-8) point out that disclosures of the defected Soviet spy, Oleg Penkovsky (E-10) are essential, claiming Penkovsky's data permitted the CIA to accurately interpret photos of the Cuban missiles.

Intelligence failures during the Cuban crisis prompted Wohlstetter (E-13) to compare Pearl Harbor and Cuba. Moser's article (E-9) is a narrative of U-2 intelligence gathered by that aircraft from 1954 to 1962. Arnold (E-1) claims American planners based the nation's security needs on Soviet capabilities rather than its intentions because of the lack of satisfactory intelligence such as in the 1962 crisis. Gleichauf (E−4), a retired CIA officer, reports on the intelligence data about Cuba secured from Cuban exiles.

E−1 Arnold, Joseph C. "Omens and Oracles." *United States Naval Institute Proceedings* 106 (Aug. 1980), 47−53.

E−2 Burnham, James. "Intelligence on Cuba." *National Review* 13 (Nov. 20, 1962), 587.

E−3 "Extent of the Cuban Missile Threat Revealed: Photo−Intelligence Briefing by Defense Secretary Robert S. McNamara and John Hughes." *Aviation Week and Space Technology* 78 (Feb. 11, 1963), 31.

E−4 Gleichauf, Justin F. "Red Presence in Cuba: The Genesis of a Crisis." *Army* 29 (Nov. 1979), 34−38.

E−5 Katz, Amon H. *The Soviets and the U−2 Photos*. Santa Monica, CA: Rand Corp., Mar. 1963.

E−6 Knorr, Klaus. "Failure in National Intelligence Estimates: The Case of the Cuban Crisis." *World Politics* 16 (Apr. 1964), 455−467.

E−7 Krock, Arthur. *Memoirs*. New York: Funk & Wagnalls, 1968.

E−8 Laird, Melvin. "Why We Need Spies." *Reader's Digest* 144 (Mar. 1979), 87−92.

E−9 Moser, Don. "The Time of the Angel: The U−2, Cuba and the CIA." *American Heritage* 28 (Oct. 1977), 4−15.

E−10 Penkovsky, Oleg Valdimirovich. *The Pankovsky Papers*. Trans. by Peter Deriabin. Garden City, NY: Doubleday, 1965.

E-11 U.S. Congress Senate Committee on Armed Services Subcommittee on Preparedness. 88th Cong., 1st Sess. *Interim Report on Cuban Military Buildup*. Washington, DC: G.P.O., 1963.

E-12 U.S. Department of Defense. *Special Cuba Briefing, February 6, 1963*. Washington, DC: G.P.O., 1963.

E-13 Wohlstetter, Roberta. "Cuba and Pearl Harbor: Hindsight and Foresight." *Foreign Affairs* 43 (July 1965), 691-707.

F. *U.S. Missiles in Turkey*

Allison (A-2) called attention to the Turkish missile situation, suggesting that previous orders to remove the missiles had not been carried out. Research by Hafner (F-3) and Bernstein (F-2) conclude that Kennedy must have known the missiles were in Turkey, because his admininstration had decided in 1961-1962 to proceed with their deployment. The ExCom transcripts (T-18) for October 16 also indicate that the Turkish situation was discussed with Kennedy on the first day after the Soviet missiles were found. On the U.S. problem in getting missiles deployed in Europe, Armacost's study (F-1) should be consulted.

Harris (F-3) has examined U.S.-Turkish relations after World War II including data on the missile issue between 1957 and 1962. Ball's memoirs (M-48) explain his involvement with the Turkish missiles before the 1962 crisis; his view agrees with Hafner and Bernstein, below.

F-1 Armacost, Michael. *The Politics of Weapons Innovation: The Thor-Jupiter Controversy*. New York: Columbia University Press, 1965.

F-2 Bernstein, Barton J. "The Cuban Missile Crisis: Trading the Jupiters in Turkey?" *Political Science Quarterly* 95 (Spring 1980), 97-125.

F-3 Hafner, Donald L. "Those Frigging Missiles: JFK, Cuba and U.S. Missiles in Turkey." *Orbis* 21 (Summer 1977), 307-334.

F—4 Harris, George. *Troubled Alliance: Turkish—American Problems in Historical Perspective 1945—1971*. Washington, DC: Brookings Institution, 1972.

G. *Cuban "Blockade" and International Law*

Scholars of international law have carefully examined the legal aspects of Kennedy's quarantine tactic in 1962. Chayes (G—1, G—2, G—3), a State Department counselor in 1962, states the Kennedy Administration's view that the quarantine was justified as a regional self—defense act of the U.S. with the Organization of American States. In the July 1963 issue of the *American Journal of International Law* (G—8), Chayes' views were defended by Christol and Davis, Fenwick, Meeker, McDougal, and MacChesney, but challenged by Wright. Defenders of the Kennedy policy used the term "quarantine" as being different from blockade; quarantine meaning the interdiction of the delivery of offensive weapons which might upset the status quo. In addition to Wright, Chayes' concepts were disputed by Gerberding (G—4) and Shalom (G—6). After Nathan (M—28) asserted that the Kennedy action caused a decline in the value of international law, Piper (G—5) defended the policy as a filling of a gap in the legal order. Travis (G—7) compares the 1956 Suez crisis with the 1962 episode, arguing that politicians manipulate international law to serve national purposes.

G—1 Chayes, Adam. *The Cuban Missile Crisis: International Crises and the Role of Law*. New York: Oxford University Press, 1974.

G—2 Chayes, Adam. "Law and the Quarantine of Cuba." *Foreign Affairs* 41 (Apr. 1963), 550—557.

G—3 Chayes, Adam. "The Legal Case for U.S. Action on Cuba." *Department of State Bulletin* 97 (Nov. 19, 1962), 763—765.

G-4 Gerberding, William P. "International Law and the Cuban Missile Crisis." In Lawrence Scheinman and David Wilkinson, eds. *International Law and Political Crisis: An Analytical Casebook.* Boston: Little, Brown, 1968, pp. 175-211.

G-5 Piper, Don C. "The Cuban Missle Crisis and International Law: Precipitous Decline or Unilateral Development." *World Affairs* 138 (Summer 1975), 26-31.

G-6 Shalom, Stephen R. "International Lawyers and other Apologists: The Case of the Cuban Missile Crisis." *Polity* 12:1 (1979), 83-109.

G-7 Travis, John Turner. "The Functions of Law in International Crisis." Ph.D. Diss., University of Arizona, 1974.

G-8 "U.S. Quarantine of Cuba, October 1962." *American Journal of International Law* 57 (July 1963), 515-592.

H. *United Nations' Role*

From October 23 until the Soviet missiles were withdrawn from Cuba, the Kennedy Administration looked to the United Nations as one means for gaining world support for the quarantine solution. In addition, the good offices of UN Secretary General U Thant were used. U Thant (H-3, H-4) explained his role in a November 1962 speech and, later, as a portion of his memoirs.

A summary of the U.N. efforts including the role of Ambassadors Stevenson and Zorin are contained in Gardner's essay (H-2) in the *U.S. State Department Bulletin* and in the *United Nations' Review* (H-1). Stevenson's activity is described by his biographer, Martin (M-42). The speeches of Stevenson (L-16) and Zorin (L-18) have also been published. Wilcox (H-5) discusses the use of the OAS as a regional bloc within the UN charter, concluding that regional blocs are seldom effective.

H-1 "Efforts to Negotiate a Peaceful Settlement." *U.N. Review* 9 (Nov. 1962), 14-15.

H-2 Gardner, R. N. "The U.N. in Crisis: Cuba and the Congo." *U.S. Department of State Bulletin* 48 (Apr. 1, 1963), 477-481.

H-3 U Thant. "The Cuban Affair: Negotiation and Compromise the Only Course." *Vital Speeches* 29 (Nov. 15, 1962), 76-77.

H-4 U Thant. *View from the U.N.* Garden City, NY: Doubleday, 1978.

H-5 Wilcox, Francis O. "Regionalism and the United Nations." *International Organization* 19 (Summer 1965), 789-811.

H-6 "U.N. Security Council Hears U.S. Charges of Soviet Buildup." *U.S. Department of State Bulletin* 47 (Nov. 19, 1962), 723-740.

I. *OAS Activity*

On October 23, the U.S. appealed to the Organization of American States to support the blockade and rally the Western Hemispheric nations against the Soviet missile challenge. Studies by Slater (I-5) and Parkinson (Q-10) deal with the Cuban crisis in relation to the broader developments of America's relations in the Western Hemisphere. The Hammarskjold Forum of the New York Bar Association (I-1) has published a survey report of OAS action during the Cuban crisis, while *Current History* (I-3, I-4) printed various resolutions passed by the OAS during the crisis. Hilton (I-2) questioned the unanimity of the OAS, claiming the U.S. used economic coercion to gain votes.

I-1 Hammarskjold Forum. *The Inter-American Security System and the Cuban Crisis.* Dobbs Ferry, NY: Association of the Bar of the City of New York, 1964.

I-2 Hilton, Ronald. "A Note on Latin America." *Council for Correspondence Newsletter*, no. 21, October 1962, 42-44.

I-3 "The OAS Resolution on Cuba (Oct. 23, 1962)" *Current History* 44 (Feb. 1963), 111 ff.

I-4 "Resolutions of the OAS Condemning Cuba in OAS Official Records." *Current History* 48 (Jan. 1965), 40-44.

I-5 Slater, Jerome. *The OAS and U.S. Foreign Policy.* Columbus: Ohio State University Press, 1967.

J. *Canada and the Crisis*

Friction arose in American relations with Canada as a result of the Cuban crisis. Accounts by Lyon (J-2) and Redford (J-3) give details of Prime Minister John Diefenbaker's concern because Washington failed to consult Canada. Ghent (J-1) explores the unsatisfactory relationship between Kennedy and Diefenbaker which the Cuban crisis heightened.

J-1 Ghent, Jocelyn Maynard. "Canada, the United States, and the Cuban Missile Crisis." *Pacific Historical Review* 48 (May 1979), 159-184.

J-2 Lyon, Peyton V. *Canada in World Affairs.* Toronto: Oxford University Press, 1968.

J-3 Redford, Robert. *Canada and Three Crises.* Lindsey, Ontario: John Deyell, 1968.

K. *Europe and the Crisis*

The Kennedy Administration hoped to pursue stronger efforts in the Third World by stabilizing the Cold War in Europe. This so-called Grand Design for U.S. policy in Europe was not successful and, as Costigliola (K-4) indicates, Kennedy's failure to consult his NATO allies during the Cuban crisis contributed to European leaders' dislike of the policy.

Studies on U.S. policy toward Europe which include information on the Cuban situation are those of Barnet (K-2), Grosser (K-6), and Newhouse (K-9). Harris (F-4) deals with U.S.-Turkish policy, while Nunnerly (K-10) examines American-British relations. A Rand Corporation study (K-3) deals with British attitudes during the Cuban crisis; Julien (K-7) summarizes world news opinion concerning Kennedy and Castro.

The memoirs of three important European leaders reflect on U.S. policy during the Cuban crisis--Konrad Adenauer (K-1), Charles DeGaulle (K-5), and Harold Macmillan (K-8).

K-1   Adenauer, Konrad. *Erinnerungen 1959-1963 Fragmente*. 4 vols. Stuttgart: Deutsche Verlag-Anstalt, 1968.

K-2   Barnet, Richard J. *The Alliance*. New York: Simon & Schuster, 1983.

K-3   *British Attitudes in the Cuban Crisis*. Santa Monica, CA: Rand Corp., 1963.

K-4   Costigliola, Frank. "The Failed Design: Kennedy, DeGaulle, and the Struggle for Europe." *Diplomatic History* 8 (Summer 1984), 227-251.

K-5   DeGaulle, Charles. *Memoirs of Hope: Renewal and Endeavor*. New York: Simon & Schuster, 1971.

K-6   Grosser, Alfred. *The Western Alliance*. Trans. by Michael Shaw. New York: Continuum, 1980.

K-7   Julien, Claude. "Kennedy-Castro." *Atlas* 5 (Mar. 1963), 177-178.

K-8   Macmillan, Harold. *At the End of the Day, 1960-1963*. New York: Harper & Row, 1973.

K-9 Newhouse, John. *DeGaulle and the Anglo–Saxons*. New York: Viking, 1970.

K-10 Nunnerly, David. *President Kennedy and Britain*. New York: St. Martin's, 1972.

L. *Documents on the Crisis*

A variety of documents and speeches for the period of the crisis are available in printed or microfilm editions. Both the Facts on File (A-6) and the Department of State (A-9) studies have general chronological accounts of Cuban–American relations from 1959 through 1962. Publications of a variety of documents regarding the crisis of 1962 have been edited by the Foreign Policy Association (L-3), Larson (L-12), and LaFeber (L-15).

President Kennedy's public papers (L-6) include his messages during the crisis period. Nevins (L-7) edited a collection of John Kennedy's speeches as part of the 1960 campaign materials. Johnson (L-4) has edited the press conferences of President Kennedy. The exchange of messages between Kennedy and Khrushchev were published in 1973 by the State Department (L-13).

Nikita Khrushchev's December 1962 report to the Supreme Soviet has been published in at least four sources (L-2, L-9, L-10, L-14); Khrushchev's November speech on the crisis is also available (L-11). The *Current Digest of the Soviet Press* (L-1) has printed various Soviet news reports on the crisis. Ronald Pope (L-14) edited a collection of both Soviet News reports and Khrushchev's statements on the crisis.

Other available documents include the speeches of Dean Rusk (M-40), Adlai Stevenson (L-16), U Thant (H-4), and Valerian Zorin (L-18). *Current History* (I-3, I-4) has printed the OAS resolutions on Cuba. Finally, Paul Keraris' microfilm edition (L-8) of CIA Research reports includes various intelligence documents on Cuba including the October 1962 U-2 information.

L-1 "Cuba: From Protests to the Removal of Soviet Missiles." *Current Digest of the Soviet Press* 14 (Nov. 21, 1962), 3-15.

L-2   Dallin, A., ed. "Khrushchev's Report to the Supreme Soviet of the U.S.S.R." In *Diversity of International Communism: A Documentary Report*. New York: Columbia University Press, 1963.

L-3   Foreign Policy Association. *The Cuban Crisis: A Documentary Record*. No. 157. New York: Headline Series, 1963.

L-4   Johnson, George W., ed. *The Kennedy Presidential Press Conferences*. New York: Coleman, 1978.

L-5   Kennedy, John F. "Arms Quarantine of Cuba: The Soviet Military Buildup." [Address to American television audience] *Vital Speeches* 29 (Nov. 15, 1962), 66-68.

L-6   Kennedy, John F. *Public Papers of the President, 1961-1963*. 3 vols. Washington, DC: G.P.O., 1962-1964.

L-7   Kennedy, John F. *The Strategy of Peace*. Ed. by Allan Nevins. New York: Harper & Row, 1960.

L-8   Kesaris, Paul, ed. "CIA Research Reports: Latin America, 1946-1976." Frederick, MD: University Publications of America, 1982. (Microfilm)

L-9   Khrushchev, Nikita. "Khrushchev's Report on the International Situation." *Current Digest of the Soviet Press* 14 (Jan. 16, 1963), 3-8.

L-10 Khrushchev, Nikita. *The Present International Situation and the Foreign Policy of the Soviet Union: Report by N.S. Khrushchev to the Supreme Soviet of the U.S.S.R.* New York: Cross-Currents Press, 1963.

L-11 Khrushchev, Nikita. "Rockets over Cuba: A Symbolic Declaration." *Current Digest of the Soviet Press* 12 (Nov. 30, 1960), 6-7.

L-12 Larson, David, ed. *The Cuban Crisis of 1962: Selected Documents and Chronology*. Boston: Houghton Mifflin, 1963.

L-13 "Messages Exchanged by President Kennedy and Chairman Khrushchev during the Cuban Missile Crisis of October 1962." *U.S. Department of State Bulletin* 69 (Nov. 19, 1973), 635-655.

L-14 Pope, Ronald R. *Soviet Views on the Cuban Missile Crisis: Myth and Reality on Foreign Policy Analysis.* Lanham, MD: University Press of America, 1982.

L-15 Schlesinger, Arthur M. Jr., ed. *The Dynamics of World Power: A Documentary History of United States Foreign Policy, 1945-1973.* Vol. 2: *Eastern Europe and the Soviet Union*, ed. by Walter LaFeber. New York: Chelsa House, 1973.

L-16 Stevenson, Adlai. "The Cuba Crisis: A Base for Communist Aggression." *Vital Speeches* 29 (Nov. 15, 1962), 70-76.

L-17 "Tass Statement on Aid to Cuba and U.S. Provocations." *Current Digest of the Soviet Press* 14 (Oct. 10, 1962), 13-15.

L-18 Zorin, V. A. "Has the U.S.S.R. Missiles in Cuba?" *Vital Speeches* 29 (Nov. 15, 1962), 77-83.

PARTICIPANTS IN THE 1962 CRISIS

The most important accounts by participants in the 1962 crisis are those of Robert Kennedy (M-34), Theodore Sorensen (M-7) and Nikita Khrushchev (N-5, N-6). Robert Kennedy's *Thirteen Days* is the only one to deal solely with the crisis and, of course, is an "inside-the-White-House" account. The most balanced biography of President Kennedy is by Parmet (M-4). Schlesinger, who served in the Kennedy Administration, has used many archival sources, not yet available to all scholars, to write his biography of Robert Kennedy (M-35). Competent biographies of Khrushchev have been written by Crankshaw (N-2) and Frankland (N-3).

M. *Americans*

(John F. Kennedy)

Most papers at the Kennedy Library are not yet available on an unrestricted basis to the general scholar. The library has been making "sanitized" (censored) versions of some documents available, including the NSC ExCom files (T−19) and the October 16, 1962, sanitized transcript of recordings (T−18) made during the two ExCom sessions. Printed sources of Kennedy's public statements are discussed in the documents sections above (see items L−4 through L−7 and L−13).

President Kennedy's role in 1962 has received the most scrutiny because much information is available on American decisions. Subsequently, studies of Kennedy's policies have been divided into two basic categories: one group tending, as did most initial accounts, to praise Kennedy; and a second "revisionist" group which has criticized Kennedy for his strong military response to the crisis. Kennedy's critics on the right have not produced significant analytical studies to verify their charges.

Studies emphasizing Kennedy's skill, courage, and successful crisis−management follow the pattern set by the memoirs of participants in the crisis such as Sorensen (M−7), Schlesinger (M−5), Hilsman (M−53), Bundy (M−50), and Robert Kennedy (M−34). Stuart (M−32) strikes a more balanced perspective on Kennedy's decision−making, associating Kennedy's can−do action with his belief in a president's need to project a strong appearance. In addition to Parmet's biography, O'Donnell and Powers (M−2) is laudatory while the study of Burner and West (M−1) is balanced favorably toward Kennedy. Schlesinger's (M−5) inside account of Kennedy's 1000 days sets the tone for the popular version of the Cuban crisis as Kennedy's "finest hour". Hargrove (R−29) and Bundy (M−50) also emphasize the president's skillful use of power during the missile crisis. Paper (M−3) sought to respond to Kennedy's critics but acknowledged that Kennedy did not achieve what he hoped. Van DeMark's (T−15) review essay favorably assessed Kennedy without substantive data.

Some scholars who originally supported Kennedy's policies, have since qualified their assessments of the president's tough stance against Russia. Allison's 1972 article (M−18) on Kennedy's "macho" image indicated the president was more cautious than previously thought, a view Schlesinger recently accepted (M−35). Similarly, Catudel (M−8) emphasizes Kennedy's caution during the Berlin Wall crisis; Patrick

(M−30) describes his flexibility in the 1961 Laotian crisis; Etzioni (M−23) explains his resiliency in seeking to move toward detente policies with Khrushchev; and Paterson (M−29) indicates Kennedy's difficulty in dealing with the Soviets. Other "not−so−tough" perspectives on Kennedy can be found in George (M−24) relating JFK's "carrot−and−stick" policies toward Khrushchev, and Monger (M−27) in explaining Kennedy's Aristotelian "golden mean" as a moderating influence on his foreign policies, particularly, in his speech for a viable balance of power with Russia.

Revisionist scholars have unearthed much data which contrasts with the favorable accounts of Kennedy's 1000 days and some which supplements the left's criticisms as summarized by Horowitz (M−13). An early revisionist account by British author Henry Fairlie (M−9) contends that Americans confused Kennedy's hyperactivity with achievement. Heath (M−12) extended Fairlie's critical concepts to the eight years of Kennedy−Johnson policies, both foreign and domestic. Halberstam's critical, journalistic volume (M−11) provides biographical vignettes of some of "the Best and the Brightest." Fitzsimons (M−10) carries Halberstam's ideas farther, arguing that the elitist attitudes of the Kennedy advisors led them to unduly rely on the military−industrial leaders whom Eisenhower had derided in 1961. Schick (M−16) relates the Berlin crisis to the Cuban crisis, a connection which caused Kennedy to lose the confidence of both President DeGaulle of France and Chancellor Adenauer of West Germany. The failure of Kennedy's "grand design" for Europe is described by Costigliola (K−4).

Revisionists make the Cuban crisis part of a broader critique of Kennedy's Cold War policies. Szulc (M−33) describes Maxwell Taylor's 1961 report to Kennedy as grossly inadequate because it oversimplified the communist menace to the Third World. Using Szulc's thesis, Miroff (M−15) indicates how Kennedy generally renewed Cold War tensions with Russia in Berlin and Southeast Asia as well as Cuba. These interpretations are summarized by Walton (M−17) who sees Kennedy as the spokesman for counter−revolution in the Third World.

Dealing more particularly with the October missile crisis, Nathan (M−28) argues that the crisis was far from being Kennedy's "finest hour," as the crisis was resolved by luck, not the president's decisiveness. Nathan's contention of Kennedy's inadequate actions in the October crisis are given greater detail and documentation in Bernstein's series of articles (M−19, M−20, M−21, M−22).

Although LaFeber's 1973 article (M−26) on the revisionists came out too early to include the full range of criticism about Kennedy, it provides a good introduction to their attitudes. Steel (M−31, M−36) has written two reviews which criticize favorable accounts of Kennedy's policies.

Biographical Materials

M−1   Burner, David and Thomas R. West. *The Torch is Passed: The Kennedy Brothers and American Liberalism.* New York: Atheneum, 1984.

M−2   O'Donnell, Kenneth and David Powers with Joe McCarthy. *Johnny, We Hardly Knew Ye.* Boston: Little, Brown, 1972.

M−3   Paper, Lewis J. *John F. Kennedy: The Promise and the Performance.* New York: DeCapo Press, 1975.

M−4   Parmet, Herbert S. *Jack: The Struggles of John F. Kennedy* and *JFK: The Presidency of John F. Kennedy.* New York: Dial Press, 1980−1983.

M−5   Schlesinger, Arthur M., Jr. *A Thousand Days: JFK in the White House.* Boston: Houghton Mifflin, 1965.

M−6   Sorensen, Theodore. *Decision Making in the White House: The Olive Branch and the Arrows.* New York: Columbia University Press, 1963.

M−7   Sorensen, Theodore. *Kennedy.* New York: Harper & Row, 1965.

Books and Monographs

M−8   Catudel, Honore. *Kennedy and the Berlin Wall Crisis: A Case Study in U.S. Decision Making.* Berlin: Verlag, 1980.

M−9   Fairlie, Henry. *The Kennedy Promise: The Politics of Expectation.* London: Eyre Methuen, 1973.

M-10 Fitzsimons, Louise. *The Kennedy Doctrine*. New York: Random House, 1972.

M-11 Halberstam, David. *The Best and the Brightest*. New York: Random House, 1972.

M-12 Heath, Jim F. *Decade of Disillusionment: The Kennedy-Johnson Years*. Bloomington: Indiana University Press, 1975.

M-13 Horowitz, David. *Free World Colossus*. New York: Hill and Wang, 1965.

M-14 Kern, Montague, Patricia W. Levering and Ralph B. Levering. *The Kennedy Crisis: The Press, the Presidency and Foreign Policy*. Chapel Hill: University of North Carolina Press, 1984.

M-15 Miroff, Bruce. *Pragmatic Illusions: The Presidential Politics of John F. Kennedy*. New York: McKay, 1976.

M-16 Schick, Jack M. *The Berlin Crisis, 1958-1962*. Philadelphia: University of Pennsylvania Press, 1971.

M-17 Walton, Richard. *Cold War and Counter-Revolution: The Foreign Policy of John F. Kennedy*. New York: Viking, 1973.

Essays

M-18 Allison, Graham T. "Cuban Missiles and Kennedy Macho: New Evidence to Dispel the Myth." *Washington Monthly* 4 (Oct. 1972), 14-19.

M-19 Bernstein, Barton J. "Courage and Commitment: The Missiles of October." *Foreign Service Journal* 52 (Oct. 1975), 9-11 and 24-27.

M-20 Bernstein, Barton J. "The Cuban Missile Crisis." In *Reflections on the Cold War*, ed. by Lynn Miller and Ronald Pruessen. Philadelphia: Temple University, 1974, 11-142.

M-21 Bernstein, Barton J. "Kennedy Brinkmanship." *Inquiry* 2 (Apr. 1979), 19–22.

M-22 Berstein, Barton J. "Kennedy and Ending the Missile Crisis: Bombers, Inspection, and the No Invasion Pledge." *Foreign Service Journal* 56 (July 1979), 8–12.

M-23 Etzioni, Amitai. "The Kennedy Experiment." *Western Political Quarterly* 20 (June 1967), 351–80.

M-24 George, Alexander L. "The Cuban Missile Crisis," in *The Limits of Coercive Diplomacy: Laos, Cuba and Vietnam*, ed. by Alexander L. George, David K. Hall and William E. Simons. Boston: Little, Brown, 1971, 86–144.

M-25 Kateb, George. "Kennedy as Statesman." *Commentary* 41 (June 1966), 54–60.

M-26 LaFeber, Walter. "Kennedy, Johnson and the Revisionists." *Foreign Service Journal* 50 (May 1973), 31–33, 39.

M-27 Monger, Thomas M. "Personality and Decision Making: John F. Kennedy in Four Crisis Decisions." *Canadian Journal of Political Science* 2 (June 1969), 200–225.

M-28 Nathan, James A. "The Missile Crisis: His Finest Hour Now." *World Politics* 27 (Jan. 1976), 256–281.

M-29 Paterson, Thomas G. "Bearing the Burden: A Critical Look at JFK's Foreign Policy." *Virginia Quarterly Review* 54 (Spring 1978), 193–212.

M-30 Patrick, Ronald. "Presidential Leadership in Foreign Affairs: Kennedy and Laos Without Radical Revisionism." *World Affairs* 140 (Winter 1978), 245–258.

M−31 Steel, Ronald. "Cooling It." *New York Review of Books* 19 (Oct. 1972), 43−46.

M−32 Stuart, Douglas Thomas. "The Relative Potency of Leader Beliefs as a Determinant of Foreign Policy: John F. Kennedy's Operational Code." Ph.D. Diss., University of Southern California, 1979.

M−33 Szulc, Tad. "Kennedy's Cold War." *New Republic* 177 (Dec. 24, 1977), 19−21.

(Robert Kennedy)

Robert Kennedy's *Thirteen Days* (M−34) was seen as the most articulate description of administrative decision making during the 1962 crisis. Nevertheless, Steel's (M−36, M−37) critique of the book argues that U.S. intelligence failed and the president intentionally avoided any diplomatic possibilities to resolve the crisis. Schlesinger's (M−35) biography of Robert Kennedy slightly qualifies the president's triumph in 1962 while revealing that Robert Kennedy had made a personal deal with Ambassador Dobrynin to withdraw the Turkish missiles. See also Acheson's review (M−46) of *Thirteen Days*.

M−34 Kennedy, Robert. *Thirteen Days: A Memoir of the Cuban Missile Crisis*. New York: Norton, 1969.

M−35 Schlesinger, Arthur S. Jr. *Robert F. Kennedy and His Times*. Boston: Houghton Mifflin, 1978.

M−36 Steel, Ronald. "Endgame, Thirteen Days." *New York Review of Books* 12 (Mar. 13, 1969), 15−22.

M−37 Steel, Ronald. "The Kennedy Fantasy." *New York Review of Books* 15 (Nov. 19, 1970), 3−12.

(Dean Rusk)

Complementing Halberstam's (M−11) comments that Rusk was chosen as Secretary of State to permit Kennedy to dominate foreign policy, Cohen (M−38) depicts Rusk as the "loyal" secretary serving his leader's policy and, consequently, not an effective factor during the missile crisis. Rusk's speech before the OAS on October 23 has been printed (M−40). In 1982, Rusk and others who had participated in the crisis prepared comments on the "lessons" of the crisis for *Time* magazine (M−39). Otherwise, Rusk has remained publically silent about his role in the 1962 affair. In 1963, a collection of Rusk's speeches (M−41) were printed for the period of 1961−62.

M−38 Cohen, Warren J. *Dean Rusk*. Totowa, NJ: Cooper Square, 1980.

M−39 Rusk, Dean, *et al.* "The Lessons of the Cuban Missile Crisis." *Time* 120 (Sept. 27, 1982), 85.

M−40 Rusk, Dean. "Missile Sites in Cuba: Offensive Purpose Against the Hemisphere." *Vital Speeches* 29 (Nov. 15, 1962), 68−70.

M−41 Rusk, Dean. *Winds of Freedom*. Boston: Beacon, 1963.

(Adlai Stevenson)

The initial Alsop−Bartlett article (B−1) on the crisis was particularly notable because it described participants as "hawks" and "doves" and symbolized Adlai Stevenson as appeasement oriented in contrast with Kennedy's toughness. Stevenson was incensed at the Alsop article and considered resigning unless President Kennedy denied the Alsop story. At the time, both Steele (M−44) and Severeid (M−43) sprang to Stevenson's defense. As Stevenson biographer John B. Martin (M−42) explains, Kennedy equivocated but others convinced Adlai he should not resign. Most accounts consider Stevenson's role in the UN confrontation with Valerian Zorin as being of excellent value. His speech (L−16) on Cuba was printed on November 15, 1962. Other of Stevenson's papers and speeches as Ambassador to the United Nations may be found in volumes 7 and 8 of his papers (M−45).

M−42 Martin, John Bartlow. *Adlai Stevenson and the World*. Garden City, NY: Doubleday, 1977.

M−43 Severeid, Eric. "The Final Troubled Hours of Adlai Stevenson." *Look* 29 (Nov. 30, 1965), 81−86.

M−44 Steele, John L. "The Adlai Stevenson Affair." *Life* 24 (Dec. 14, 1962), 44−46.

M−45 Stevenson, Adlai E. *The Papers of Adlai E. Stevenson*. 8 vols. Ed. by Walter Johnson. Boston: Little, Brown, 1972−1979.

(Other Americans)

In addition to Sorensen and Robert Kennedy, members of the ExCom who have published memoirs are General Maxwell Taylor (M−61, M−62) and George Ball (M−48); while Secretary of Defense Robert McNamara (M−58) and McGeorge Bundy (M−50) have written brief accounts of their views. Accounts by persons who attended a few ExCom sessions or gave Kennedy advice include Dean Acheson's article (M−46), which claimed that "luck" won the day on October 28, and memoirs by Charles Bohlen (M−49), Curtis LeMay (M−57) and Roger Hilsman (M−53, M−54). Arthur Schlesinger Jr. (M−5) became Kennedy's court historian and his account of these years is partly memoir, partly an "inside" story. Schlesinger revised his ideas slightly in 1983 (M−35). Hilsman (M−53, M−54, M−55) wrote a book and an article as well as engaging in controversy with Steel on the crisis. Finally, Senator Kenneth Keating (M−56) explained his role during the crisis.

Other studies worth consulting for the period are Richard Nixon's (M−59) account of the 1960 campaign; Adam Yarmolinsky's (M−64) report of Defense Department operations in the 1962 crisis; and the reports by Anderson (M−47) and Caldwell (M−51) on Navy action in October 1962. Welch (M−63) contrasts the hard−line views of Adolf Berle in 1962 with those of Walter Lippmann. Steel (M−60) indicates that Kennedy admired but seldom followed Lippmann's advice.

M−46 Acheson, Dean. "Dean Acheson's Version of Robert Kennedy's Version of the Cuban Missile Affairs: Homage to Plain Dumb Luck." *Esquire* 71 (Feb. 1969), 44, 76.

M-47 Anderson, Admiral George W., Jr. "The Navy and the Decision-Making Process in Diplomatic Crisis." *Proceedings of a U.S. Naval History Symposium* (Annapolis, MD: U.S. Naval Academy, 1973).

M-48 Ball, George W. *The Past Has Another Pattern: Memoirs.* New York: W. W. Norton, 1982.

M-49 Bohlen, Charles E. *Witness to History, 1929-1969.* New York: W. W. Norton, 1973.

M-50 Bundy, McGeorge. "The Presidency and the Peace." *Foreign Affairs* 42 (Apr. 1964), 353-365.

M-51 Caldwell, Dan. "A Research Note on the Quarantine of Cuba, October 1962." *International Studies Quarterly* 22 (Dec. 1978), 625-633.

M-52 Harriman, W. Averell. *America and Russia in a Changing World: A Half Century of Personal Observations.* Garden City, NY: Doubleday, 1971.

M-53 Hilsman, Roger. "The Cuban Crisis: How Close We Were to War." *Look* 28 (Aug. 25, 1964), 17-21.

M-54 Hilsman, Roger. *To Move A Nation.* Garden City, NY: Doubleday, 1967.

M-55 Hilsman, Roger and Ronald Steel. "An Exchange of Views." *New York Review of Books* 12 (May 8, 1969), 17-21.

M-56 Keating, Kenneth. "My Advance View of the Cuban Crisis." *Look* 28 (Nov. 3, 1964), 96-106.

M-57 LeMay, Curtis E. *America is in Danger.* New York: Funk & Wagnalls, 1968.

M−58 McNamara, Robert. "Red Missiles in Cuba: An Inside Story From Secretary McNamara." *U.S. News and World Report* 53 (Nov. 5, 1962), 44−50.

M−59 Nixon, Richard M. *Six Crises.* Garden City, NY: Doubleday, 1962.

M−60 Steel, Ronald. *Walter Lippmann and the American Century.* New York: Random House, 1980.

M−61 Taylor, Maxwell D. *Responsibility and Response.* New York: Harper & Row, 1967.

M−62 Taylor, Maxwell D. *Swords and Ploughshares.* New York: Norton, 1962.

M−63 Welch, Richard E. Jr. "Lippmann, Berle, and the U.S. Response to the Cuba Revolution." *Diplomatic History* 6 (Spring 1982), 125−143.

M−64 Yarmolinsky, Adam. "Department of Defense Operations During the Cuban Crisis." Edited by Dan Caldwell in *Naval War College Review* 32 (July−Aug. 1979), 83−99.

N. *The Soviet Union*

Nikita Khrushchev's memoirs (N−5, N−6) cover all of his career including the 1962 crisis. In addition, Khrushchev's official reports on the crisis and its aftermath are published in several editions (L−2, L−9, L−10, L−14). And, Valerian Zorin's UN speech on the missiles is printed in *Vital Speeches* (L−18). The messages Kennedy and Khrushchev exchanged in October 1962, were published by the State Department (L−13).

(Nikita Khrushchev)

Roy Medvedev (N−8), a Soviet writer whose works are smuggled out of Russia for publication in the West, published a biography of Khrushchev which gives insights into the Russian leader's conflicts with colleagues in the Politiburo during the early 1960's. Frankland (N−3) believes Soviet missiles were placed in Cuba as a gamble to reduce Russia's inferiority in strategic missiles. Wedge's essay (N−9) is a report which Wedge, a social psychiatrist, sent to Kennedy in 1961 prior to the Vienna Conference. Khrushchev's relationship within the Soviet system is explored by Linden (N−7), Crankshaw (N−2), and Burg and Wiles (N−1). Hyland and Shryrock (N−4) explain Khrushchev's fall from leadership in 1964.

N−1 Burg, D. and P. Wiles. "Khrushchev's Power Position−−Polycentrism within the Soviet Ruling Group." In *The Soviet Political Process*, ed. by S. I. Ploss. Waltham, MA: Ginn, 1971.

N−2 Crankshaw, Edward. *Khrushchev: A Career*. New York: Viking, 1966.

N−3 Frankland, Mark. *Khrushchev*. New York: Stein & Day, 1967.

N−4 Hyland, W. and R. W. Shryrock. *The Fall of Khrushchev*. New York: Funk & Wagnalls, 1968.

N−5 Khrushchev, Nikita S. *Khrushchev Remembers*. Trans. by Strobe Talbott with commentary by Edward Crankshaw. Boston: Little, Brown, 1976.

N−6 Khrushchev, Nikita S. *Khrushchev Remembers: The Last Testament*. Trans. and ed. by Strobe Talbott. Boston: Little, Brown, 1974.

N−7 Linden, C. A. *Khrushchev and the Soviet Leadership, 1957−1964*. Baltimore: Johns Hopkins Press, 1966.

N−8 Medvedev, Roy. *Khrushchev: A Biography*. Garden City, NY: Doubleday, 1983.

N−9 Wedge, Bryant. "Khrushchev at a Distance−−A Study of Public Personality." *Trans−action* 5 (Oct. 1968), 24−28 and 6 (Dec. 1968), 63−64.

(Other Russians)

Accounts of the Cuban crisis by Soviet writers generally discount the activity of individuals involved. Their views, however, may be found in Anatolli Gromyko's (A−7, A−14) accounts and in articles by Igor Statsenko (A−17) and A. Schevechenko (N−10). Zorin's speech at the UN was printed on November 15, 1962 (L−18). *Newsweek* (N−11) reported that the younger Gromyko's original article was a defense of his father's role during the crisis.

Pope has edited with commentary (L−14) four major Soviet accounts of the crisis, including Khrushchev's December 1962 report. Both Dinerstein (P−3) and Scherer (P−12) use Soviet news reports and editorials in order to analyze Soviet viewpoints.

N−10 Schevechenko, A. *"Bon Voyage, Cuban Friends." Current Digest of Soviet Press* 15 (Oct. 9, 1963), 21.

N−11 *"Son's Defense: Kremlin Issues Official Version." Newsweek* 78 (Aug. 9, 1971), 111−112.

O. *Cubans*

While Draper (O−3, O−4) is critical of Castro, two sympathetic works are Mills (Q−19) and Matthews (O−7, O−8) who interviewed Castro during his revolutionary years in the Sierra Maestra's from 1955−1958. Castro's rise to power against Batista's government is described by Dorschner and Fabricio (Q−15). Franqui's (O−5) first−hand account gives detailed insights into both the fight against Batista and Castro's rejection by Cuban communists before 1959. Halperin (O−6) examines both Castro's rise to power and his declining influence, relating the latter to his inability to solve that nation's economic problems.

Castro's own statements (O−2) on the missile crisis and his discussions with U.N. Secretary General U Thant are collected in a volume published by the Cuban government. Other writings by Castro before, during and after the crisis are listed in Bonachea's annotated bibliography (O-1). In interviews with Szulc (O-9) in early 1984, Castro added recollections to his previous accounts of the Cuban crisis. Castro claimed the missiles were the Soviet's idea and that the weapons were always controlled by Soviet officers in 1962.

O-1 Bonachea, Rolando. *A Briefly Annotated Bibliography of Fidel Castro's Works, 1959-1970*. Pittsburgh: University of Pittsburgh, Center for International Studies, 1973.

O-2 Castro, Fidel. *Atlas Armas*. Havana: Govierno Municipal Revolucionario, 1963.

O-3 Draper, Theodore. *Castroism: Theory and Practice*. New York: Praeger, 1965.

O-4 Draper, Theodore. *Castro's Revolution: Myths and Realities*. New York: Praeger, 1962.

O-5 Franqui, Carlos. *Diary of the Cuban Revolution*. New York: Viking, 1980.

O-6 Halperin, Maurice. *The Rise and Decline of Fidel Castro: An Essay in Contemporary History*. Berkeley: University of California Press, 1972.

O-7 Matthews, Herbert. *The Cuban Story*. New York: Braziller, 1962.

O-8 Matthews, Herbert L. *Fidel Castro*. New York: Simon & Schuster, 1969.

O-9 Szulc, Tad. "Castro on John Kennedy and the Missile Crisis." *Los Angeles Times*, April 15, 1984, Part IV, 1 and 3.

NATIONAL DIMENSIONS

P. *The Soviet Dimension*

Although Soviet behavior is difficult to describe or analyze because of inadequate source materials, scholarly efforts to evaluate Soviet motivations and decisions are important. Two of the best general studies of Soviet political processes under Khrushchev's regime have been written by Tatu (P−14) and Kolkowicz (P−11). Kolkowicz (P−9, P−10) prepared two other studies on relations between "hawks" and "doves" within the Soviet political system for the Rand Corporation. Of only slightly less value for the 1962 crisis are studies by Horelick (P−5) and by Horelick and Rush (P−6). Kaplan (P−8) has published a long−term assessment of Soviet concerns with foreign powers armed against their regime since the pre−1917 years.

(Soviet Policy Making)

Both Tatu (P−14) and Kolkowicz (P−11) explain the divergent pressures on Khrushchev within the Kremlin as a vital part in understanding Soviet decision−making. Two excellent works on Soviet policy which emphasize the late 1940's and early 1950's are by Dallin (S−5) and Jackson (P−7). Ulam (P−15) deserves special mention as an articulate and insightful explanation of Soviet activity. The biographies of Khrushchev by Frankland (N−3) and Medvedev (N−8) both deal with Soviet policy during the missile crisis; the former contending that Khrushchev was striving to gain nuclear parity with America.

Several studies consider the national security aspects of the Soviet decision on Cuba. Theberge (P−23) investigates Moscow's naval strategy and activity with reference to the Caribbean. Bloomfield (S−3) describes Soviet arms construction policy during the decade following Stalin's death. Hodgson (P−4) concludes that the Kremlin's basic motive in defense preparations, including placing missiles in Cuba, was to protect the U.S.S.R. from attack by the capitalist nations. Somewhat similarly, George and Smoke (R−4) indicate that the Soviets considered the decision to place missiles in Cuba as a low−risk situation which would enchance their defenses in Europe. Smolansky (P-13) contends that Khrushchev's motive in Cuba was to catch up with America's nuclear superiority. In contrast, Wolfe (P-16) stresses the Berlin issue as the Kremlin's principal motive in Cuba.

Six studies examine the historical circumstances which motivated the Soviet decision to place missiles in Cuba. Kolkowicz, *et. al.* (S-11) explores Soviet considerations of whether arms control or an arms race would best serve their national security. Horelick and Rush (P-6) concluded that U.S. exposure of Soviet missile inferiority in 1961 prompted Khrushchev's decision to place missiles in Cuba. Cottrell (P-1) deals with the Soviet belief that America's NATO bases were intended for provocative U-2 flights or a surprise attack on the U.S.S.R. Using content analysis of Soviet and Cuban documents, Dinerstein (P-3) devises interesting insights into the Kremlin's decisions on Guatemala during 1954 and Cuba from 1959 to 1962. Crosby (P-2) contends the Soviet Union sought to gain a power balance with the U.S. by placing missiles in Cuba. The circumstances of the two letters to Washington on October 26 and 27 are analyzed by Scherer (P-12).

P-1 Cottrell, Alvin J. "Soviet Views of U.S. Overseas Bases." *Orbis* 7 (Spring 1963), 77-95.

P-2 Crosby, Ralph. "The Cuban Missile Crisis--The Soviet View." *Military Review* 56 (Sept. 1976), 58-70.

P-3 Dinerstein, Herbert S. *The Making of a Missile Crisis: October 1962*. Baltimore: Johns Hopkins University Press, 1976.

P-4 Hodgson, John H. "Soviet Foreign Policy: Mental Alienation or Universal Revolution." *Western Political Quarterly* 24 (Dec. 1971), 653-665.

P-5 Horelick, Arnold D. "The Cuban Missile Crisis: An Analysis of Soviet Calculations and Behavior." *World Politics* 16 (Apr. 1964), 363-389.

P−6 Horelick, Arnold D. and Myron Rush. *Strategic Power and Soviet Foreign Policy*. Chicago: University of Chicago Press, 1965.

P−7 Jackson, William D. "The Soviets and Strategic Arms: Toward an Evaluation of the Record." *Political Science Quarterly* 94 (Summer 1979), 243−261.

P−8 Kaplan, Stephen S. *Diplomacy of Power: Soviet Armed Forces and Political Instrument*. Washington, DC: Brookings Institution, 1981.

P−9 Kolkowicz, Roman. *Conflicts in Soviet Party−Military Relations: 1962−1963*. Santa Monica, CA: Rand Corp., 1963.

P−10 Kolkowicz, Roman. "The Red Hawks on the Rationality of Nuclear War." Santa Monica, CA: Rand Memorandum RM−4899−PR, 1966.

P−11 Kolkowicz, Roman. *The Soviet Military and the Communist Party*. Princeton: Princeton University Press, 1967.

P−12 Scherer, John L. "Reinterpreting Soviet Behavior during the Cuban Missile Crisis." *World Affairs* 144 (Fall 1981), 110−125.

P−13 Smolansky, Oles M. "Moscow and the Cuban Missile Crisis: Reflections on Khrushchev's Brinkmanship." *Politico* 33 (Sept. 1968), 509−526.

P−14 Tatu, Michel. *Power in Kremlin: From Khrushchev to Kosygin*. Trans. by Helen Katel. New York: Viking, 1969.

P−15 Ulam, Adam. *Expansion and Coexistence: The History of Soviet Foreign Policy*. New York: Praeger, 1968.

P−16 Wolfe, Thomas W. *Soviet Power and Europe, 1945−1970*. Baltimore: Johns Hopkins, 1970.

(Soviet—Cuban Relations)

Two studies which relate Soviet—Cuban relations to the broader context of Latin American policies of the superpowers have been written by de Madariaga (P−21) and Parkinson (Q−10). Blaiser (P−17) focuses on Soviet policies in Latin America.

Gonzales (P−19) analyzes Moscow's responses to Havana's appeals for aid. Both Tretiak (P−24) and Burks (P−18) deal generally with Soviet assistance to Castro after 1959. Suarez (Q−21), a former official in Castro's government, explains the shifts in Cuban policies which aligned Castro with communism between 1958 and 1961. Jackson (P−20) investigates the Kremlin's use of Castroism to spread communism throughout Latin America. A *U.S. State Department Bulletin* (P−29) described the Soviet military build−up in Cuba by early 1962, while Navarro (P−22) analyzes the various types of Soviet armaments in Cuba. Theberge (P−23) describes the build−up of Soviet naval forces in the Caribbean area.

P−17 Blaiser, Cole. *The Giant's Rival: The U.S.S.R. in Latin America*. Pittsburgh: University of Pittsburgh Press, 1983.

P−18 Burks, David. *Soviet Policy for Castro's Cuba*. Columbus: Ohio State University Press, 1964.

P−19 Gonzales, Edward. "Castro's Revolution: Cuban Commmunist Appeals and the Soviet Response." *World Politics* 21 (Oct. 1968), 29−68.

P−20 Jackson, Bruce. *Castro, the Kremlin and Communism in Latin America*. Baltimore: Johns Hopkins University Press, 1969.

P−21 Madariaga, Salvador de. *Latin America Between the Eagle and the Bear*. New York: Praeger, 1962.

P−22 Navarro, M. *An Analysis of Soviet Reasons for the Military Buildup in Cuba*. Maxwell A.F.B., AL: Air University Library, 1964.

P−23 Theberge, James D. *Soviet Seapower in the Caribbean: Political and Strategic Implications.* New York: Praeger, 1972.

P−24 Tretiak, Daniel. "Cuba and the Soviet Union: the Growing Accomodation, 1964−1965." *Orbis* 11 (Summer 1967), 439−458.

(Sino−Soviet Relations and the Crisis)

The Chinese−Soviet relations with regard to the Cuban crisis are reviewed in three divergent studies. Mao's backing for Cuba, even to the extent of a war with America is indicated in the *Peking Review's* survey (P−25) of China's official announcements. Crane's article (P−26) relates the Cuban situation to the contest for Third World status between Peking and Moscow. Dapondes (P−27) examines the relationship of the Cuban crisis to the Chinese−Indian border war which broke out on October 20, 1962.

More general aspects of the Sino−Soviet dispute may be found in studies by Griffith (P−28). Tang and Maloney (P−30) describe China's efforts to influence Cuba.

P−25 "All Out Support for Cuba." *Peking Review* 5 (Nov. 9, 1962), 11.

P−26 Crane, Robert D. "The Sino−Soviet Dispute on War and the Cuban Crisis." *Orbis* 8 (Fall 1964), 537−549.

P−27 Dapondes, Andrew. *The Cuban Crisis and the Chinese−Indian Border War.* New York: Vantage, 1968.

P−28 Griffith, William E. *The Sino−Soviet Rift.* Cambridge: Harvard University Press, 1964.

P−29 "Sino−Soviet Block Military Aid to Cuba Summarized." *U.S. Department of State Bulletin* 46 (Apr. 16, 1962); 644−646.

P−30 Tang, Peter S. H. and Joan Maloney. *The Chinese Communist Impact on Cuba*. Chestnut Hill, MA: Research Institute on the Sino−Soviet Bloc, 1962.

Q. *The Cuban Dimension*

Thomas (Q−13) has written a monumental study of Cuban history which is valuable for understanding developments in that island. Another useful, general account of Cuba is the volume by Barnett and McGaffey (Q−1).

(United States, Cuba and the Caribbean)

In addition to studies of U.S.−Cuban relations from 1959−1962, students should become familiar with the broader history of Washington's policy in Latin America and the Caribbean. Perez (T−12) has an excellent historiographical article on American policy in the Caribbean from 1898 to 1980. Langley (Q−5, Q−6) and Martin (Q−9) are useful surveys of American relations in the Caribbean; while Crassweiler (Q−4) emphasizes the persistent difficulties in American−Cuban relations. More detailed studies of the fall of Batista and rise of Castro are the dissertations by Bonachea (Q−3) and Tierney (Q−14).

Two studies with somewhat different conclusions on U.S. intervention practices in the Caribbean have been written by Perkins (Q−12) and Pearce (Q−11). Perkins' official−style study seeks to justify U.S. intervention; while Pearce opposes U.S. intervention, blaming Washington for supporting obsolete regimes in the area. Blasier (Q−2) and Lipson (Q−7) describe America's Cold War interventions in Latin America.

Three studies investigate inter−American relations preceding the 1962 crisis. Slater (I−5) explains Washington's efforts to use the Organization of American States to foster U.S. policy; while Parkinson (Q−10) studies Latin American developments during the super−powers Cold War relations from 1945 to 1973. In 1964, the Hammarskjold Forum (I−1) described inter−American security during the Cuban crisis of the early 1960's.

In 1975, Senator George McGovern toured Cuba to investigate if the U.S. and the OAS should end the economic embargo against Castro. McGovern's report (Q−8) covered all aspects of U.S. relations with Cuba since 1959 and recommended that America should seek to improve its relationship with the Castro regime.

Q-1 Barnett, Clifford and Wyatt McGaffey. *Twentieth Century Cuba: The Background of the Castro Revolution*. Garden City, NY: Doubleday, 1965.

Q-2 Blasier, Cole. *The Hovering Giant: United States Responses to Revolutionary Change in Latin America*. Pittsburgh: University of Pittsburgh Press, 1976.

Q-3 Bonachea, Rolando E. "United States Policy Toward Cuba: 1959–1961." Ph.D. Diss., Georgetown University, 1976.

Q-4 Crassweiler, Robert D. *Cuba and the U.S.: Their Tangled Relationship*. New York: Foreign Policy Association, 1971.

Q-5 Langley, Lester D. *The United States and the Caribbean, 1900–1970*. Athens: University of Georgia Press, 1980.

Q-6 Langley, Lester D. *The Cuban Policy of the United States: A Brief History*. New York: Wiley, 1968.

Q-7 Lipson, Leon. "Castro on the Chessboard of the Cold War." In *Cuba and the United States*, ed. by John Plank. (Washington, DC: Brookings Institution, 1967), 178–199.

Q-8 McGovern, Senator George. *Cuban Realities: May 1975*. Report to the committee on Foreign Relations, United States Senate. Washington, DC: G.P.O., 1975, p. 14.

Q-9 Martin, John Bartlow. *U.S. Policy in the Caribbean*. Boulder, CO: Westview, 1978.

Q-10 Parkinson, F. *Latin America, the Cold War, and the World Powers, 1945–1973*. Beverly Hills, CA: Sage, 1974.

Q-11 Pearce, Jenny. *Under the Eagle: U.S. Intervention in Central America and the Caribbean*. Boston: South End Press, 1982.

Q-12 Perkins, Whitney T. *Constraint of Empire: The United States and Caribbean Interventions*. Westport, CT: Greenwood, 1981.

Q-13 Thomas, Hugh. *Cuba: The Promise of Freedom*. New York: Harper & Row, 1971.

Q-14 Tierney, Kevin Beirne. "American-Cuban Relations: 1957-1963." Ph.D. Diss., Syracuse University, 1979.

(The United States and Castro)

Commentaries by participants and historical studies are controversial regarding Batista's fall and Castro's victory in 1959. American diplomats Berle (C-2) and Bonsal (C-3) blame the Eisenhower Administration; while Smith (C-6) believes the State Department's Latin American Division prematurely wrote off Batista. Welch (Q-22) examines the relationship between Herbert Matthews of the *New York Times* and Castro.

Mills (Q-19) and Lowenthal (Q-18) blamed American policy for not understanding Cuban developments. Williams (Q-23) believes neither Eisenhower, Kennedy, nor other U.S. policymakers comprehended the revolutionary nationalism of Cuba, a failure that forced Castro to turn to Moscow for aid. Johnson (Q-16) believes that concern for U.S. business interests in Cuba prevented Washington's leaders from dealing properly with Castro. Lazo (Q-17) has written a critical polemic of U.S. policy in Cuba.

Robbins (Q-20) believes the U.S. has constantly overestimated the Cuban threat to America and the Western Hemisphere. Suarez (Q-21), a former Cuban official under Castro, sees Fidel as a skillful politician. The most balanced account of Batista's fall is the study by Dorschner and Fabricio (Q-15). Two doctoral dissertations (Q-3, Q-14) have undertaken an analysis of Cuba and the U.S. between 1959 and 1962.

Q-15 Dorschner, John and Roberto Fabricio. *The Winds of December*. New York: Coward, McCann, 1980.

Q-16 Johnson, Leland L. "U.S. Business Interests in Cuba and the Rise of Castro." *World Politics* 17 (Apr. 1965), 440-459.

Q-17 Lazo, Mario. *Dagger in the Heart: American Foreign Policy Failures in Cuba.* New York: Funk & Wagnells, 1968.

Q-18 Lowenthal, David. "U.S.-Cuban Policy: Illusion and Reality." *National Review* 14 (Jan. 29, 1963), 61-63.

Q-19 Mills, C. Wright. *Listen, Yankee.* New York: McGraw-Hill, 1960.

Q-20 Robbins, Carla Anna. *The Cuban Threat.* New York: McGraw-Hill, 1983.

Q-21 Suarez, Andres. *Cuba, Castroism and Communism, 1959-1966.* Trans. by Joel Carmichael and Ernst Halperin. Cambridge: MIT Press, 1967.

Q-22 Welch, Richard E., Jr. "Herbert L. Matthews and the Cuban Revolution." *The Historian* 47 (Nov. 1984), 1-18.

Q-23 Williams, William A. *The U.S., Cuba and Castro: An Essay in the Dynamics of Revolution and the Dissolution of Empire.* New York: Monthly Review Press, 1962.

(Kennedy, the CIA and Castro)

Kennedy's use of the CIA in various actions against Cuba were disclosed by the U.S. Senate's investigation of that intelligence agency in the mid-1970's. The Senate findings (Q-25) were published in 1975 and formed the basis for an article by Branch and Crile (Q-24) which described Kennedy's "vendetta" against Castro. CIA briefings (Q-26) on Cuba for the Senate Foreign Policy Committee were general in nature, not disclosing information later discovered in 1975.

Q-24 Branch, Taylor and George Crile III. "The Kennedy Vendetta: How the CIA Waged a Silent War Against Cuba." *Harpers Magazine* 251 (Aug. 1975), 49-63.

Q-25 U.S. Congressional Senate Select Committee to Study Governmental Operations. *Alleged Assassination Plots Involving Foreign Leaders.* 94th Cong., 1st Sess. Washington DC: G.P.O., 1975.

Q-26 U.S. Senate. *Executive Sessions of the Senate Foreign Relations Committee* (Historical Series), Vol. XII. 86th Cong., 1960. Washington, DC: G.P.O., 1982.

(Bay of Pigs Episode)

The Bay of Pigs invasion and other Kennedy policies toward Castro in 1961 and early 1962 are examined by Crassweiler (Q-4) and Robbins (Q-20). Crassweiler explains the difficult problems between Washington and Havana; Robbins emphasizes the tendency of Kennedy and other U.S. presidents to exaggerate Cuba's threat. Three valuable studies on the Bay of Pigs are: Meyer and Szulc's (Q-32) account of the failure; Johnson's (Q-30) study based on interviews with the Cuban exiled leaders of the invasion; Wyden's (Q-34) excellent examination of the invasion; and Hunt's (Q-29) approval of this effort to overthrow Castro.

The recent release of documents has raised questions regarding Kennedy's decisions on the Bay of Pigs. The Taylor Report on the inquiry into the disaster has been declassified and edited by Kesaris (Q-31). Bissell (Q-27) has disclosed data in preparation for the invasion. Vandenbroucke (Q-33) wrote an analysis of Allen Dulles' unpublished memoir which brought a rejoinder from Bissell (Q-28). The point at issue is the relations between Kennedy and CIA planners.

Q-27 Bissell, Richard M. Jr. "Reflections on the Bay of Pigs." *Strategic Review* 12 (Winter 1984), 69-70.

Q-28 Bissell, Richard M. Jr. "Response to Lucien S. Vandenbroucke." *Diplomatic History* 8 (Fall 1984), 377-380.

Q-29 Hunt, Howard. *Give Us This Day*. New York: Arlington House, 1973.

Q-30 Johnson, Haynes, et. al. *The Bay of Pigs: The Leaders Story of Brigade 2506*. New York: Norton, 1964.

Q-31 Kesaris, Paul L., ed. "Operation Zapata: The 'Ultrasensitive' Report and Testimony of the Board of Inquiry on the Bay of Pigs." Frederick, MD: University Publications of America, 1981. (Microfilm)

Q-32 Meyer, Karl Ernest and Tad Szulc. *The Cuban Invasion*. New York: Praeger, 1962.

Q-33 Vandenbroucke, Lucien S. "The Confessions of Allen Dulles: New Evidence on the Bay of Pigs." *Diplomatic History* 8 (Fall 1984), 365-375.

Q-34 Wyden, Peter. *Bay of Pigs: The Untold Story*. New York: Simon & Schuster, 1979.

NATIONAL SECURITY DIMENSIONS

R. *Deterrence Theory*

Students of deterrence theory have profited from studying the 1962 crisis because the two superpowers risked potential nuclear war. In an excellent introductory essay, Jervis (R-6) noted that deterrence is part of the broader theory of coercive diplomacy but, since the missile crisis, deterrence has entered the popular vocabulary. Smoke (P-17) indicates the Cuban crisis also made "escalation" part of that vocabulary.

The Cuban crisis occurred at a time when deterrence theorists emphasized the "chicken" game model. Such commentators as Brodie (R-1) and Schelling (R-13) argued that the two sides would initially stand firm during a confrontation. From a firm stance, the two sides would manipulate tactics such as feigning anger, acting irrational, cutting communications, or advancing steps short of war which would eventually coerce one opponent to back away from the brink of nuclear war. Rusk's comment near the end of the October 1962 crisis summarized Kennedy's victory as "they blinked first" in an "eyeball–to–eyeball" confrontation.

Soon after the Cuban crisis ended, and partly as a result of that crisis, deterrence scholars moved to a more sophisticated stage of analysis. Beginning with Russett's essay (R−11) on "The Calculus of Deterrence", studies of international relations by George and Smoke (R−4), Fink (R−2), Kecskemeti (R−8), Morgan (R−10), Snyder and Diesing (R−15), Young (R−16), and George, Hall and Simons (R−3) criticized the shortcomings of previous deterrence theory. They also proposed new studies based on such factors as comparative empirical evidence, negotiations which include positive rewards and compromise, and consideration of the risks involved in a crisis or of things which could go wrong when the "chicken model" was followed.

The general theories of deterrence may be reviewed in two valuable introductory volumes by Schelling (R−12) and Holsti (R−5). A more complex discussion of escalation is contained in the study of Kahn (R−7). In 1981, Lebow (R−9) described deterrence as an international condition which is neither peace nor war.

R−1 Brodie, Bernard. *Strategy in the Missile Age*. Princeton: Princeton University Press, 1959.

R−2 Fink, Clinton. "More Calculations About Deterrence." *Journal of Conflict Resolution* 9 (Mar. 1965), 54−65.

R−3 George, Alexander, David K. Hall and William E. Simons, eds. *The Limits of Coercive Diplomacy: Laos, Cuba and Vietnam*. Boston: Little, Brown, 1971.

R−4 George, Alexander and Richard Smoke. *Deterrence in American Foreign Policy*. New York: Columbia University Press, 1974.

R−5 Holsti, Ole R. *Crisis, Escalation, War*. Montreal: McGill Queen's University Press, 1972.

R-6 Jervis, Robert. "Deterrent Theory Revisited." *World Politics* 31 (Jan. 1979), 314-322.

R-7 Kahn, Herman. *On Escalation*. New York: Praeger, 1965.

R-8 Kecskemeti, Paul. *Strategic Surrender*. New York: Athenlum, 1964.

R-9 Lebow, Richard N. *Between Peace and War: The Nature of International Crisis*. Baltimore: Johns Hopkins University Press, 1981.

R-10 Morgan, Patrick. *Deterrence*. Beverly Hills: Sage, 1977.

R-11 Russett, Bruce. "The Calculus of Deterrence." *Journal of Conflict Resolution* 7 (June 1963), 97-109.

R-12 Schelling, Thomas. *Arms and Influence*. New Haven: Yale University Press, 1966.

R-13 Schelling, Thomas C. *The Strategy of Conflict*. Cambridge: Harvard University Press, 1960.

R-14 Smoke, Richard. "Theories of Escalation," in Paul G. Lauren, ed. *Diplomacy*. New York: Free Press, 1979, pp. 162-182.

R-15 Snyder, Glenn and Paul Diesing. *Conflict Among Nations*. Princeton: Princeton University Press, 1977.

R-16 Young, Oran R. *The Politics of Force*. Princeton: Princeton University Press, 1968.

(Deterrence Studies in the 1962 Crisis)

In applying theoretical deterrent concepts, scholars have developed studies relating the Cuban crisis to such previous events as Sarajevo-1914, Munich-1938, and Korea-1950 — see Paige (R-22), Holsti

(R−17), Lockhart (R−19) and Mendenhall (R−20). In another study, Holsti and Brody (R−18) analyzed data from the Cuban crisis alone. Using data from comparative studies, Moisi (R−21) contends that the 1962 crisis was most valuable because it involved two powers with nuclear capabilities.

R−17 Holsti, Ole R. "Theories of Crisis Decision Making." In Paul Gordon Lauren, ed. *Diplomacy.* New York: Free Press, 1979, pp. 99−136.

R−18 Holsti, Ole R. and R. A. Brody. "Measuring Affect and Action in International Reaction Models: Empirical Materials from the 1962 Cuban Crisis." *Peace Research Society* 2 (Oct. 1965), 170−190.

R−19 Lockhart, Charles. "The Varying Fortunes of Incremental Commitment: An Inquiry into the Cuban and Southeast Asian Cases." *International Studies* 1:3 (1974), 14−21.

R−20 Mendenhall, Warner DeWitt. "The Concept of United States Crisis Management in the Bi−Polar World." Ph.D. Diss., Kent State University, 1982.

R−21 Moisi, Dominique. "Analogy as Temptation: Understanding the Present International Crisis." *Social Research* 48 (Winter 1981), 739−748.

R−22 Paige, G. D. "Comparative Case Analysis of Crisis Decisions: Korea and Cuba." In *International Crisis: Insights from Behavioral Research.* New York: Free Press, 1972, pp. 41−55.

(Leader Behavior and the Decision Process)

The behavior of leaders during crises is the focus of several studies. Stuart (M−32), Janis (R−31), Lockhart (R−32), Anderson (R−23), and Sullivan (R−36) have examined the leaders' statements which committed them to escalation in a crisis. George (R−27) describes the president's use of force during the 1962 crisis. Steinberg (R−35) believes the incompatible goals of the superpowers caused the escalation of threats.

Some analysts gave particular attention to the American decision—making process, paralleling Allison's (A−2) three categories. Destler (R−25) studies inter−agency forces which played a role in Washington's decisions. Erwin Hargrove (R−29, R−30) analyzes the decision powers and limitations on the president. George (R−26, R−28) studies the value of group advocacy in the decision process and indicates that policy makers must consider the codes of belief influencing each nation. President Kennedy's flexibility in 1962 both in using force and in signaling concessions to Moscow is emphasized in studies by Allison (M−18), Cowhey and Laitin (R−24), and by George (M−24).

In contrast to studies which stressed the escalation of threat during the 1962 crisis, accounts by the Wohlstetters (R−37) and Holsti and Brody (R−18) emphasize that war was avoided because Washington and Moscow both combined the application with the relaxation of force. Rapoport (R−33, R−34) used his model of two−person game theory to analyze the perceptions of U.S. and Soviet leaders in various crises.

R−23 Anderson, Paul A. "Justifications and Precedents as Constraints in Foreign Policy Decision−Making." *American Journal of Political Science* 25 (Nov. 1981), 738−761.

R−24 Cowhey, Peter F. and David D. Laitin. "Bearing the Burden: A Model of Presidential Responsibility." *International Studies Quarterly* 22 (June 1978), 267−296.

R−25 Destler, I. M. *Presidents, Bureaucrats, and Foreign Policy.* Princeton: Princeton University Press, 1974.

R−26 George, Alexander, L. "The Case for Multiple Advocacy in Making Foreign Policy," with comments by I. M. Destler and a rejoiner by the author. *American Political Science Review* 66 (Sept. 1972), 751−795.

R−27 George, Alexander L. *Presidential Control of Force: The Cuban Missile Crisis.* Santa Monica, CA: Rand Corp., July 1967.

R-28 George, Alexander L. "The Operational Code: A Neglected Approach to the Study of Political Leaders and Decision-Making." *International Studies Quarterly* 13 (June 1969), 190-222.

R-29 Hargrove, Erwin C. *The Power of the Modern Presidency.* New York: Knopf, 1974.

R-30 Hargrove, Erwin C. "Presidential Personality and Revisionist Views of the Presidency." *American Journal of Political Science* 17 (Nov. 1973), 819-835.

R-31 Janis, Irving L. *Victims of Groupthink: A Psychological Study of Foreign Policy Decisions and Fiascos.* Boston: Houghton Mifflin, 1972.

R-32 Lockhart, Charles. "Problems in the Management and Resolution of International Conflicts." *World Politics* 29 (Apr. 1977), 370-403.

R-33 Rapoport, Anatol. *The Big Two: Soviet-American Perceptions of Foreign Policy.* New York: Pegasus, 1971.

R-34 Rapoport, Anatol. *Two-Person Game Theory: The Essential Ideas.* Ann Arbor: University of Michigan Press, 1966.

R-35 Steinberg, Blema S. "Goals in Conflict: Escalation, Cuba 1961." *Canadian Journal of Political Science* 14 (Mar. 1981), 83-105.

R-36 Sullivan, Michael P. "Commitment and the Escalation of Conflicts." *Western Political Quarterly* 25 (Mar. 1972), 28-38.

R-37 Wohlstetter, Albert and Roberta. *Controlling the Risks in Cuba.* Adelphi Paper 43. London: International Institute for Strategic Studies, 1965. Also published in *The Use of Force: International Politics and Foreign Policy*, ed. by Robert J. Art and Kenneth N. Waltz. Boston: Little, Brown, 1971.

S. *Consequences of the Cuban Crisis*

The Cuban missile crisis has been viewed as a watershed in U.S.–Soviet relations. In 1982, two articles summarized some of the legacies of October 1962. Dean Rusk, Robert McNamara, George Ball, Roswell Gilpatric, Theodore Sorensen and McGeorge Bundy (S–17) listed five lessons of the crisis. Pollard (S–14) summarized the events to assess the lessons about management learned during the crisis.

This essay will consider the influence of the Cuban crisis in terms of four historical developments: (1) the superpowers' move toward detente and arms control; (2) the renewed Soviet–American military build–up; (3) the search for better methods to manage or deter future nuclear confrontation; and (4) the clarification of the precise pledges agreed to by Kennedy and Khrushchev on October 28.

(Detente and Arms Control)

Between 1963 and 1976, American policy shifted gradually from policies of Cold War confrontation toward an era of consultation (detente) and attempts to reach arms limitation agreements with the Soviet Union. Peterson (S–13) finds Kennedy's inauguration of steps to relax the U.S. agricultural embargo of the U.S.S.R. led to an increase of trade between the superpowers over the next twenty years. Saito (S–18) suggests that the era from Sputnik in 1957 through the Cuban crisis forced a change in U.S. assumptions of its military–technical omnipotence. Sakamoto (S–19) correctly predicted in 1968 that the 1962 crisis moved the U.S. to consider principles of peaceful coexistence with communism, a change which would lead the U.S. to accept the People's Republic of China in 1971.

Other scholars such as Dean (S–6), Bader (S–2), Rodman (S–15), Helde (S–8) and Hayden (S–7) emphasize that near nuclear war in 1962 led Washington and Moscow to move toward arms control as part of detente. Paul Boyer (S–4) describes how the American public shifted from the great fear of nuclear tests and war in the early 1960's to apathy about the nuclear issue until 1980. This process was aided by arms agreements after 1962, beginning with the 1963 Test Ban Treaty and continuing through the signing of SALT I and SALT II. These changes resulted, in part, from the American policy which accepted some degree of nuclear parity with the Soviets, a policy explained by Jacobs (S−9), Rossi (S−16), Anderson (S−1), Sullivan (S−21), and Hodgson (P−4).

There are several studies on arms control which are associated with 1962. Seaborg (S−20) offers an inside view of the negotiations leading to the 1963 Test Ban Treaty. Ball (D−2) describes the Kennedy Administration's change from an initial "panic" attempt to attain U.S. nuclear superiority in 1961 to recognition that a grant of some degree of nuclear parity to the Soviet Union was aided by the "comfortable" Western superiority in total ICBM's and conventional weapons.

Bloomfield, Clemens and Griffiths (S−3) examine the factors limiting an arms build−up in the U.S.S.R. during the decade after Stalin's death. Jonsson (S−10) believes the Cuban crisis was a major event in the formation of the 1963 Test Ban Treaty. Dallin (S−5) and Kolkowicz (S−11) discuss the Soviet views and debates about whether arms control or an arms race would be best for Soviet security. Newhouse (S−12) examines the U.S.−Soviet negotiations leading to the signing of the Strategic Arms Limitations Treaties of 1972.

S−1 Anderson, Stephen S. "United States−Soviet Relations: The Path to Accommodation." *Current History* 55 (Nov. 1968), 281−287.

S−2 Bader, William B. *The United States and the Spread of Nuclear Weapons*. New York: Pegasus, 1968.

S−3 Bloomfield, Lincoln P., Walter Clemens, and Franklyn Griffiths. *Khrushchev and the Arms Race: Soviet Interests in Arms Control and Disarmament, 1954−1964*. Cambridge: MIT Press, 1966.

S−4 Boyer, Paul. "From Activism to Apathy: The American People and Nuclear Weapons, 1963−1980." *Journal of American History* 70 (Mar. 1984), 821−844.

S−5 Dallin, Alexander, et. al. *The Soviet Union and Disarmament: An Appraisal of Soviet Attitudes and Intentions*. New York: Praeger, 1964.

S-6 Dean, Arthur H. *The Test Ban and Disarmament: The Path of Negotiation.* New York: Harper & Row, 1966.

S-7 Hayden, Eric W. "Soviet–American Arms Negotiations, 1960–1968: A Prelude to Salt." *Naval War College Review* 24:5 (1972), 65–82.

S-8 Helde, Thomas T. "The Kennedy–Johnson Years." *Current History* 57 (July 1969), 31–35.

S-9 Jacobs, Walter Darnell. "Soviet Strategic Effectiveness." *Journal of International Affairs* 26:1 (1972), 60–72.

S-10 Jonsson, Christer. *Soviet Bargaining Behavior: The Nuclear Test Ban Case.* New York: Columbia University Press, 1979.

S-11 Kolkowicz, Roman, et. al. *The Soviet Union and Arms Control: A Superpower Dilemma.* Baltimore: Johns Hopkins University Press, 1970.

S-12 Newhouse, John. *The Cold Dawn: The Story of SALT.* New York: Holt, Rinehart & Winston, 1973.

S-13 Peterson, Trudy Huskamp. "Sales, Surpluses, and the Soviets: A Study of Political Economy." *Policy Science Journal* 6 (Summer 1978), 531–533.

S-14 Pollard, Robert A. "The Cuban Missile Crisis: Legacies and Lessons." *Wilson Quarterly* 6 (Autumn 1982), 148–158.

S-15 Rodman, Peter W. "The Missiles of October: Twenty Years Later." *Commentary* 74 (Oct. 1982), 39–45.

S-16 Rossi, Mario. "Les relations Americano–Sovietiques." *Politique Etrangere* [France] 41:5 (1976), 423–432.

S-17 Rusk, Dean, et al. "The Lessons of the Cuban Missile Crisis." *Time* 120 (Sept. 27, 1983), 85.

S-18 Saito, Makoto. "A New Beginning for American Diplomacy." *Journal of Social and Political Ideas in Japan* I:1 (1963), 83-86.

S-19 Sakamoto, Yoshikazu. "Reverse the Course of History by Force?" [Reverser par la Force le Cours de l'histoire?] *Guerres et Paix* 3 (1968), 9-19.

S-20 Seaborg, Glenn T. *Kennedy, Khrushchev and the Test Ban*. Berkeley: University of California Press, 1981.

S-21 Sullivan, Robert R. "ABM, MIRV, SALT and the Balance of Power." *Midwest Quarterly* 13 (Oct. 1971), 11-36.

S-22 Thomas, Brian. "What's Left of the Cold War?" *Political Quarterly* 4 (April-June 1969), 173-186.

(Renewed Military Build-up)

Although the superpowers sought detente and arms control after 1962, they also continued their military construction programs. In the view of some military analysts, the West had lost its superiority relative to the U.S.S.R. by 1979. Gallois (S-25) described the relative American decline following the 1962 crisis, arguing that Anglo-French cooperation should try to retain a favorable European nuclear balance. Collins (S-23), Jacobs (S-9), and Foster (S-24) contended the West's weakness antedated the Cuban crisis.

Allegations of Moscow's move toward superiority by the Committee on the Present Danger helped to generate sufficient popular American fears to cause the U.S. Senate to avoid action on the 1979 SALT II treaty. Prados (S-28) and Sanders (S-29) describe the activity of this committee and its success in renewing the Cold War by 1980.

Hamilton (S-26) examines the declining influence of the JCS after 1962, as civilians gained more authority in the White House, the NSC and the Defense Department. The reversal of this decline after 1975 is described by Korb (S-27).

S−23 Collins, John M. *American and Soviet Military Trends Since the Cuban Missile Crisis*. Washington, DC: Georgetown University Press, 1978.

S−24 Foster, John. "The Growing Soviet Threat−−A Sobering Picture." *Air Force and Space Digest* 53:11 (1970), 77−81.

S−25 Gallois, Pierre. "1967−1972." *Politique Etrangere* [France] 37 (1972), 29−64.

S−26 Hamilton, William A., III. "The Decline and Fall of the JCS." *Naval War College Review* 25 (Apr. 1972), 47.

S−27 Korb, Lawrence J. *The Fall and Rise of the Pentagon: American Defense Policies in the 1970's*. Westport, CT: Greenwood, 1979.

S−28 Prados, John. *The Soviet Estimate*. New York: Dial, 1982.

S−29 Sanders, Jerry W. *Peddlers of Crisis: The Committee on the Present Danger and the Politics of Containment*. Boston: South End, 1983.

S−30 Ullman, Harlan. "The Cuban Missile Crisis and Soviet Naval Development: Myths and Realities." *Naval War College Review* 28 (Winter 1976), 45−56.

(Search for a Better Way to Handle a Crisis)

Following the Cuban crisis, a number of scholars and commentators concluded that the conduct of the two superpowers during a crisis should be improved. Christianson (S−34) and Paper (S−40) deplored the use of nuclear threats to resolve disputes and one leader's ability to determine the fate of millions of people. Kateb (M−25) pointed out that although the Kennedy Administration had good intentions, White House advisors oversimplified the use of face−saving and prestige−gaining assumptions. Similarly, Joxie (S−37) argued that the perception that Kennedy achieved "victory" by managing an escalation of threat caused American policy−makers to use force in the Dominican Republic and Vietnam in 1965.

Other aspects of shortcomings of American decision—making were examined by Lebow (S−38) and Sugden (S−41). Lebow described the irrationality of Kennedy's "testing of the will" attitude and concluded that the U.S. learned the wrong lessons from the Cuban crisis. Sugden described how Kennedy's use of the news media during October 1962 influenced the decisions being made during the crisis.

Using a global perspective to seek a better method to handle a crisis, Borch (S−33) advocated the formation of a special group within the Western alliance to handle future nuclear confrontations. Neuchterlein (S−39) examined U.S. relations with such Third World nations as Cuba, arguing that Americans needed to clarify the relationship of such nations to U.S. security. Bell (S−31) included events of the Cuban crisis in describing tactics to be used during a crisis. Jervis (S−36) indicated that the leader's image of himself and his nation influence decisions during a crisis. Ekman (S−35) argued that a leader's statements before a crisis were often used to justify, perhaps in error, his acts during a crisis. Likewise, Bernstein (S−32) concluded that prior commitments were followed during a crisis even though the circumstances required a change in policy.

S−31 Bell, Carol. *The Conventions of Crisis: A Study in Diplomatic Management.* London: Oxford University Press, 1971.

S−32 Bernstein, Barton J. "Courage and Commitment: The Missiles of October." *Foreign Service Journal* 52 (Oct. 1975), 9−11, 24−27.

S−33 Borch, Herbert von. "Glanz un elend des crisis management," ["The glory and misery of crisis management"]. *Aussenpolitik.* [West Germany] 18 (1967), 258−278.

S−34 Christianson, Gale Edward. "Nuclear Tyranny and the Divine Rights of Kings." *Bulletin of the Atomic Scientists* 27 (Jan. 1971), 44−46.

S−35 Ekman, Paul, *et. al.* "Coping with Cuba: Divergent Policy Preferences of State Political Leaders." *Journal of Conflict Resolution* 10 (June 1966), 180−197.

S-36 Jervis, R. *The Logic of Images in International Relations*. Princeton: Princeton University Press, 1970.

S-37 Joxie, Alain. "Stereotypes ou adaptation dans eu politique exterieure des Etats-Unis," ["Stereotypes or adaptation in the foreign policy of the United States"]. *Politique Etrangere* [France] 30 (1965), 173-193.

S-38 Lebow, Richard N. "The Cuban Missile Crisis: Reading the Lessons Correctly." *Political Science Quarterly* 98 (Fall 1982), 431-458.

S-39 Nuechterlein, Donald E. "The Concept of National Interest: A Time for New Approaches." *Orbis* 23:1 (1979), 73-82.

S-40 Paper, Lewis J. "The Moral Implications of the Cuban Missile Crisis." *American Scholar* 41 (Spring 1979), 276-283.

S-41 Sugden, G. Scott. "Public Diplomacy and the Missiles of October." *Naval War College Review* 24:2 (1971), 28-43.

(The Kennedy-Khrushchev Understanding)

On October 28, 1962, neither the statements of Premier Khrushchev nor those of President Kennedy were precise about the exchange of pledges by these two leaders. Kennedy's right-wing critics believed the president yielded too much in protecting Castro from overthrow. Writers such as Lazo (Q-17) and Nixon (B-19) claimed Kennedy gained no real advantage from the crisis. Because Kennedy did not mention the Turkish missiles in his October 28 announcement, scholars argued about that part of the pledges. Until publication of the studies of Schlesinger (M-35) on Robert Kennedy, of Hafner (F-3) and of Bernstein (F-2) on the Turkish missiles, the Turkish portion of the October 28 agreement was uncertain.

After 1962, at least two incidents in U.S.-Soviet-Cuban relations caused a reconsideration of the "deal" between Khrushchev and Kennedy. Both in 1970 and 1978, reports of Soviet weapons and aircraft in Cuba caused a reaction in Washington. Quester (S-43) discounts the Cuban pledge as applicable in 1970; while Garthoff (S-42) and

Bernstein (M−22) agreed that the Soviet activity in 1978 did not violate the 1962 agreement.

S−42 Garthoff, Raymond L. "American Reaction to Soviet Aircraft in Cuba, 1962 and 1978." *Political Science Quarterly* 95 (Fall 1980), 427−439.

S−43 Quester, George. "Missiles in Cuba, 1970." *Foreign Affairs* 49 (Apr. 1971), 494−506.

BASIC REFERENCES

T. *Bibiliographical and Archival Sources*

(Bibliographies)

The best bibliography of material on the 1962 crisis published to 1975, and especially good on the publications from 1963 to 1969 is by Gillingham (T−7). An invaluable guide to U.S. foreign relations including those relating to Cuba is that of Burns (T−3). Medland's (T−10) dissertation describes four categories of interpretations on the crisis: the traditional pro−Kennedy view; the right and left critics; and studies which explain Soviet behavior. Although it was published relatively early, Crown's (T−4) bibliographical essay is useful on the Kennedy literature. Van DeMark (T−15) has an annotated essay of major studies about Kennedy.

The three most valuable listings regarding the Cuban revolution are by Bonachea, (T−1); Fort (T−6); and Valdes and Lieuwen (T−14). Perez (T−12) has an excellent historiographical essay on American policy in the Caribbean. Trask (T−13) lists works dealing with U.S. relations with Latin America. Trask's volume has been supplemented by Meyer (T−11).

Other bibliographical references useful in studying the 1962 crisis include: the *Foreign Affairs Bibliography* (T−5) and each quarterly edition of that journal; Burns' (T−2) list of studies on arms control; and materials on Soviet foreign policy listed and annotated by Horecky

(T−9) for the years to 1963 and by Horak (T−8) for the period 1964 to 1974.

T−1   Bonachea, Rolando E. *Briefly Annotated Bibliography of Fidel Castro's Works, 1959−1970.* Pittsburgh: University of Pittsburgh Press, 1973.

T−2   Burns, Richard Dean. *Arms Control and Disarmament: A Bibliography.* Santa Barbara, CA: ABC−Clio, 1977.

T−3   Burns, Richard Dean, ed. *Guide to American Foreign Relations Since 1700.* Santa Barbara, CA: ABC−Clio, 1983.

T−4   Crown, James T. *The Kennedy Literature: A Bibliographical Essay on John F. Kennedy.* New York: New York University Press, 1968.

T−5   *Foreign Affairs Bibliography: A Selected and Annotated List of Books on International Relations.* 5 vols. New York: Harper, 1933−1972.

T−6   Fort, Giberto V. *The Cuban Revolution of Fidel Castro Viewed From Abroad.* Lawrence: University of Kansas Libraries, 1969.

T−7   Gillingham, Arthur. *The Cuban Missile Crisis: A Selected Bibliography.* Los Angeles: California State University, 1976.

T−8   Horak, Stephen M., ed. *Russia, The USSR and Eastern Europe: A Bibliographical Guide to English Language Publications, 1964−1974.* Littleton, CO: Libraries Unlimited, 1978.

T−9   Horecky, Paul L., ed. *Russian and Soviet Union: A Bibliographic Guide to Western Language Publications.* Chicago: University of Chicago Press, 1965.

T-10 Medland, William James. "The America–Soviet Nuclear Confrontation of 1962: An Historiographical Account." Ph.D. Diss., Ball State University, 1979.

T-11 Meyer, Michael C. *Supplement to a Bibliography of United States–Latin American Relations Since1810.* Lincoln: University of Nebraska Press, 1979.

T-12 Perez, Louis A. Jr. "Intervention, Hegemony, and Dependency: The United States in the Circum–Caribbean, 1898–1980 (Historiographical Essay." *Pacific Historical Review* 51 (May 1982), 165–194.

T-13 Trask, David W., et. al. *A Bibliography of United States–Latin American Relations Since 1810: A Selected List of 11,000 Published References.* Lincoln: University of Nebraska Press, 1968.

T-14 Valdes, Nelson P. and Edwin Lieuwen. *The Cuban Revolution: A Research–Study Guide, 1959–1969.* Albuquerque: University of New Mexico Press, 1971.

T-15 Van DeMark, Brian. "Kennedy the Diplomatist." *Newsletter* of Society for Historians of American Foreign Relations 15 (Dec. 1984), 21–34.

(Archival Sources)

Although complete documentation of the Cuban missile crisis awaits the end of the general thirty–year rule of the National Archives, some materials have been made available. As noted earlier, a microfilm copy of CIA Research Reports (L–8) is available. Caldwell (T–16) has excerpts from CIA reports between October 21 and 26; while Paterson (T–17) reprints Sorensen's October 17 memo.

Scholars using the John F. Kennedy Library, Columbia Point, Boston, Massachusetts, or the Lyndon B. Johnson Library, Austin, Texas, need to check with the respective library archivist regarding records availability. Significant sources available for the Cuban crisis at the Kennedy Library include: the sanitizied transcript of the October 16, 1962, ExCom sessions (T–18), National Security Files for the ExCom meetings (T–19), and oral history interviews of Dean Acheson,

Theodore Sorensen and Charles Bohlen. Declassified papers in the President's official file, and the Sorensen, Robert Kennedy and Arthur Schlesinger papers are also available at the Kennedy Library.

The Johnson Library has available the summaries of the ExCom sessions after October 22, 1963, in the Vice President's File.

T-16 Caldwell, Dan. *Missiles in Cuba: A Decision—Making Game.* New York: Learning Resources in International Studies, 1979.

T-17 Paterson, Thomas, ed. *Major Problems of American Foreign Policy: Vol. II Since 1914.* Lexington, MA: D.C. Heath, 1978.

T-18 Transcript of Presidential Recordings, Cuban Missile Crisis, Executive Committee of the National Security Council, Session 1 and Session 2 of October 16, 1962, sanitized revision of transcript released for use, October 1983 at the John F. Kennedy Library. The sanitizied transcripts appear to delete intelligence sources and technical military details.

T-19 Boxes 315 and 316, National Security Files, Executive Committee, especially contain memorandum and minutes of the ExCom meetings from October 23 to 31, 1962. Some of the data in these files are sanitized, some declassified and some still classified as of June 1, 1984. John F. Kennedy Library.

AUTHOR INDEX

Able, Elie: 85 (A−1)
Acheson, Dean: 111 (M−46)
Adenauer, Konrad: 100 (K−1)
Alexander, George L.: 130 (R−22)
Aliano, Richard A.: 92 (D−1)
Allison, Graham T.: 85 (A−2);
   86 (A−11); 107 (M−18)
Alsop, Stewart: 88 (B−1, B−2)
Anderson, Adm.
   George W., Jr.: 112 (M−47)
Anderson, Paul A.: 130 (R−22)
Anderson, Stephen S.: 134 (S−1)
Armacost, Michael: 95 (F−1)
Arnold, Joseph C.: 94 (E−1)
Art, Robert J.: 132 (R−37)
Ascoli, Max: 88 (B−3)

Bader, William B.: 134 (S−2)
Ball, Desmond: 92 (D−2)
Ball, George W.: 112 (M−48)
Barnet, Richard J.: 100 (K−2)
Barnett, Clifford: 123 (Q−1)
Bartlett, Charles: 86 (A−10);
   88 (B−1)
Beck, Kent M.: 91 (C−1)
Beggs, Robert: 85 (A−3)
Bell, Coral: 138 (S−31)
Berle, Adolf A., Jr.: 91 (C−2)
Bernstein, Barton J.: 86 (A−12);
   88 (B−4, B−5); 95 (F−2);
   107 (M−19, M−20);
   108 (M−21, M−22);
   138 (S−32)
Bissell, Richard M., Jr.: 126 (Q−27, Q−28)
Blaiser, Cole: 120 (P−17); 123 (Q−2)
Bloomfield, Lincoln P.: 134 (S−3)
Bolen, Charles C.: 112 (M−49)
Bonachea, Rolando E.: 116 (O−1);
   123 (Q−3); 141 (T−1)
Bonsal, Philip W.: 91 (C−3)
Borch, Herbert von: 138 (S−33)
Bottome, Edgar M.: 92 (D−3)
Boyer, Paul: 134 (S−4)
Branch, Taylor: 126 (Q−24)
Brodie, Bernard: 128 (R−1)
Brody, R. A.: 130 (R−18)
Bundy, McGeorge: 112 (M−50)

Burg, D.: 114 (N−1)
Burner, David: 106 (M−1)
Burnham, James: 94 (E−2)
Burks, David: 120 (P−18)
Burns, Richard D.: 141 (T−2, T−3)

Caldwell, Dan: 112 (M−51);
   143 (T−16)
Castro, Fidel: 116 (O−2)
Catudal, Honore: 106 (M−8)
Chase, Stuart: 88 (B−6)
Chayes, Abram: 96 (G−1, G−2, G−3)
Christianson, Gale Edward: 138 (S−34)
Clemens, Walter: 134 (S−3)
Cohen, Warren I.: 110 (M−38)
Collins, John M.: 135 (S−13)
Costigliola, Frank: 100 (K−4)
Cottrell, Alvin J.: 118 (P−1)
Cowhey, Peter F.: 131 (R−24)
Crane, Robert D.: 88 (B−1);
   121 (P−26)
Crankshaw, Edward: 114 (N−2)
Crassweiler, Robert D.: 123 (Q−4)
Crile, George, III: 125 (Q−20)
Crosby, Ralph: 118 (P−2)
Crown, James T.: 141 (T−4)

Dallin, Alexander: 102 (L−2);
   134 (S−5)
Daniel, James: 88 (B−8)
Dapondes, Andrew: 121 (P−27)
Dean, Arthur H: 135 (S−6)
DeGaulle, Charles: 100 (K−5)
Destler, I. M.: 131 (R−25)
Detzer, David: 85 (A−4)
Dewart, Leslie: 89 (B−9)
Dick, James C.: 92 (D−4)
Diesing, Paul: 129 (R−15)
Dinerstein, Herbert S.: 118 (P−3)
Divine, Robert A.: 85 (A−5)
Dorschner, John: 124 (Q−15)
Draper, Theodore: 86 (A−13);
   116 (O−3, O−4)

Ekman, Paul: 138 (S−35)
Etzioni, Amitai: 108 (M−23)

Fabricio, Roberto: 124 (Q−15)

Facts on File: 85 (A-6)
Fairlie, Henry: 106 (M-9)
Fink, Clinton: 128 (R-2)
Fitzsimons, Louise: 107 (M-10)
Foreign Policy Association: 102 (L-3)
Fort, Giberto V.: 141 (T-6)
Foster, John: 137 (S-24)
Frankland, Mark: 114 (N-3)
Franqui, Carlos: 116 (O-5)

Gallois, Pierre: 137 (S-25)
Gardner, R. N.: 98 (H-2)
Garthoff, Raymond L.: 140 (S-42)
George, Alexander L.: 108 (M-24); 128 (R-3, R-4); 131 (R-26, R-27)
Gerberding, William P.: 97 (G-4)
Ghent, Jocelyn Maynard: 99 (J-1)
Gillingham, Arthur: 141 (T-7)
Gleichauf, Justin F.: 94 (E-4)
Gonzales, Edward: 120 (P-19)
Gray, Colin S.: 93 (D-5)
Griffiths, Franklyn: 134 (S-3)
Griffith, William E.: 121 (P-28)
Gromyko, Anatolli: 85 (A-7); 86 (A-14)
Grosser, Alfred: 100 (K-6)

Hafner, Donald L.: 95 (F-3)
Hagen, Roger: 88 (B-5); 89 (B-10)
Halberstam, David: 107 (M-11)
Hall, David K.: 108 (M-24); 128 (R-3)
Halperin, Maurice: 116 (O-6)
Hamilton, William A., III: 137 (S-26)
Hammarskjold Forum: 98 (I-1)
Hargrove, Erwin: 132 (R-29, R-30)
Harriman, W. Averell: 112 (M-52)
Harris, George: 96 (F-4)
Hayden, Eric W.: 135 (S-7)
Heath, Jim F.: 107 (M-12)
Helde, Thomas T.: 135 (S-8)
Hilsman, Roger: 112 (M-53, M-54, M-55)
Hilton, Ronald: 98 (I-2)
Hodgson, John H.: 118 (P-4)
Holsti, Ole R.: 128 (R-5); 129 (R-6); 130 (R-17, R-18)
Horak, Stephan M.: 141 (T-8)
Horecky, Paul L.: 141 (T-9)
Horelick, Arnold D.: 118 (P-5); 119 (P-6)
Horowitz, David: 107 (M-13)

Hubbell, John G.: 88 (B-8)
Hunt, Howard: 127 (Q-29)
Hurwitch, Robert A.: 86 (A-15)
Hyland, W.: 114 (N-4)

Jackson, Bruce: 120 (P-20)
Jackson, William D.: 119 (P-7)
Jacobs, Walter Darnell: 135 (S-9)
Janis, Irving L.: 132 (R-31)
Jenkins, Ray: 89 (B-11)
Jervis, Robert: 129 (R-6); 139 (S-36)
Johnson, George W.: 102 (L-4)
Johnson, Haynes: 127 (Q-30)
Johnson, Leland L.: 125 (Q-16)
Johnson, Major General Max S.: 89 (B-12)
Johnson, Walter: 111 (M-45)
Jonsson, Christer: 135 (S-10)
Joxie, Alain: 139 (S-37)
Julien, Claude: 100 (K-7)

Kahan, Jerome H.: 89 (B-13)
Kahn, Herman: 129 (R-7)
Kaplan, Stephen S.: 119 (P-8)
Kateb, George: 108 (M-25)
Katz, Amron H.: 94 (E-5)
Keating, Kenneth B.: 112 (M-56)
Kecskemeti, Paul: 129 (R-8)
Kennedy, John F.: 91 (C-5); 102 (L-5, L-6, L-7)
Kennedy, Robert: 109 (M-34)
Kern, Montague.: 107 (M-14)
Kesaris, Paul: 102 (L-8); 127 (Q-31)
Khrushchev, Nikita: 102 (L-9, L-10, L-11); 114 (N-5, N-6)
Kissinger, Henry: 89 (B-14)
Knorr, Klaus: 94 (E-6)
Kolkowicz, Roman: 119 (P-9, P-10, P-11); 135 (S-11)
Korb, Lawrence J.: 137 (S-27)
Kraus, Sidney: 91 (C-4)
Krock, Arthur: 94 (E-7)

LaFeber, Walter: 108 (M-26)
Laird, Melvin: 94 (E-8)
Laitin, David D.: 131 (R-24)
Lang, Anne K.: 89 (B-13)
Langley, Lester D.: 123 (Q-5, Q-6)
Larson, David: 102 (L-12)
Lauren, Paul Gordon: 129 (R-6)
Lazo, Mario: 125 (Q-17)
Lebow, Richard N.: 129 (R-9); 139 (S-38)

LeMay, Curtis: 112 (M−57)
Levering, Patricia, W.: 107 (M−14)
Levering, Ralph B.: 107 (M−14)
Licklider, Roy E.: 93 (D−6)
Lieuwein, Edwin: 142 (T−14)
Lippman, Walter: 89 (B−15)
Linden, C. A.: 114 (N−7)
Lipson, Leon: 123 (Q−7)
Lockhart, Charles: 130 (R−19); 132 (R−32)
Lowenthal, David: 125 (Q−18)
Lyon, Peyton V.: 99 (J−2)

MacDonald, R. St. John: 98 (I−2)
McDonough, Joseph A.: 86 (A−16)
McGaffey, Wyatt: 123 (Q−1)
McGovern, Senator George: 123 (Q−8)
Mackintosh, J. Malcolm: 89 (B−16)
Macmillan, Harold: 100 (K−8)
McNamara, Robert: 113 (M−58)
Madariaga, Salvador De: 120 (P−21)
Maloney, Joan: 122 (P−30)
Martin, John Bartlow: 110 (M−42); 123 (Q−9)
Matthews, Herbert: 116 (O−7, O−8)
Medland, William James: 142 (T−10)
Medvedev, Roy: 114 (N−8)
Medenhall, Warner DeWitt: 130 (R−20)
Meyer, Karl Ernest: 126 (Q−27)
Meyer, Michael C.: 142 (T−11)
Mills, C. Wright: 125 (Q−19)
Miroff, Bruce: 107 (M−15)
Moisi, Dominique: 130 (R−21)
Monger, Thomas M.: 108 (M−27)
Morgan, Patrick: 129 (R−10)
Morgenthau, Hans J.: 89 (B−17)
Moser, Don: 94 (E−9)
Murphy, Charles J. V.: 93 (D−7)

Nathan, James A.: 108 (M−28)
Navarro, M.: 120 (P−22)
Neustadt, Richard: 89 (B−18)
Newhouse, John: 101 (K−9); 135 (S−12)
Nixon, Richard M.: 89 (B−19); 113 (M−59)
Nuechterlein, Donald E.: 139 (S−39)
Nunnerly, David: 101 (K−10)

O'Donnell, Kenneth: 106 (M−2)

Pachter, Henry: 85 (A−8)
Paige, G. D.: 130 (R−22)

Paper, Lewis J.: 106 (M−3); 139 (S−40)
Parkinson, F.: 123 (Q−10)
Parmet, Herbert S.: 106 (M−4)
Paterson, Thomas G.: 108 (M−29); 143 (T−17)
Patrick, Richard: 108 (M−30)
Pearce, Jenney: 123 (Q−11)
Penkovsky, Oleg Vladimirovich: 94 (E−10)
Perez, Louis A., Jr.: 142 (T−12)
Perkins, Whitney T.: 124 (Q−12)
Peterson, Trudy Huskamp: 135 (S−13)
Piper, Don C.: 97 (G−5)
Plank, John N.: 123 (Q−7)
Pollard, Robert A.: 135 (S−14)
Pomerance, Josephine W.: 90 (B−20)
Pope, Ronald R.: 103 (L−14)
Powers, David: 106 (M−2)
Prados, John: 137 (S−28)

Quester, George: 140 (S−43)

Rabinowich, Eugene: 90 (B−21)
Rand Corporation: 100 (K−3)
Rapoport, Anatol: 132 (R−33, R−34)
Redford, Robert: 99 (J−3)
Robbins, Carla Anna: 125 (Q−20)
Rodman, Peter W.: 135 (S−15)
Rossi, Mario: 135 (S−16)
Rush, Myron: 119 (P−6); 129 (R−7)
Rusk, Dean: 110 (M−39, 40, 41); 136 (S−17)
Russett, Bruce: 129 (R−11)

Saito, Makoto: 136 (S−18)
Sakamoto, Yoshikazu: 136 (S−19)
Sanders, Jerry W.: 137 (S−29)
Schechter, Jerold: 114 (N−2)
Schell, Jonathan: 93 (D−8)
Schelling, Thomas C.: 129 (R−12, R−13)
Scherer, John L.: 119 (P−12)
Schevechenko, A.: 115 (N−10)
Schick, Jack M.: 107 (M−16)
Schlesinger, Arthur M. Jr.: 103 (L−15); 106 (M−5); 109 (M−35)
Seaborg, Glenn T.: 136 (S−20)
Severeid, Eric: 111 (M−43)
Shalom, Stephen R.: 97 (G−6)
Shryrock, R. W.: 114 (N−4)
Simons, William E.: 108 (M−24)

Slater, Jerome: 99 (I−5)
Smith, Earl E. T.: 91 (C−6)
Smoke, Richard: 129 (R−14)
Smolansky, Oles M.: 119 (P−13)
Snyder, Glenn: 129 (R−15)
Sorensen, Theodore: 106 (M−6, M−7)
Statsenko, Igor: 86 (A−17)
Steel, Ronald: 109 (M−31, M−36, M−37); 113 (M−60)
Steele, John L.: 111 (M−44)
Steinberg, Blema S.: 132 (R−35)
Stevenson, Adlai: 103 (L−16); 111 (M−45)
Stone, I. F.: 90 (B−22, B−23)
Stuart, Douglas Thomas: 109 (M−32)
Suarez, Andres: 125 (Q−21)
Sugden, G. Scott: 139 (S−41)
Sullivan, Michael P.: 132 (R−35)
Sullivan, Robert R.: 136 (S−21)
Szulc, Tad: 109 (M−33); 116 (O−9); 127 (Q−32)

Tang, Peter: 122 (P−30)
Tatu, Michael: 119 (P−14)
Taylor, Maxwell D.: 113 (M−61, M−62)
Theberge, James D.: 121 (P−23)
Thomas, Brian: 136 (S−22)
Thomas, Hugh: 124 (Q−13)
Tierney, Kevin Beirne: 124 (Q−14)
Toledano, R.: 90 (B−24)
Trask, David W.: 142 (T−13)
Travis, John Turner: 97 (G−7)
Tretiak, Daniel: 121 (P−24)

Ulam, Adam: 119 (P−15)
Ullman, Harlan: 137 (S−30)
U Thant: 98 (H−3, H−4)
U. S. Congress, Senate Committee on Armed Services: 95 (E−11)
U. S. Congress, Senate Foreign Relations Committee: 126 (Q−26)
U. S. Congress, Senate, Select Committee to Study Governmental Operations: 126 (Q−25)
U. S. Department of Defense: 95 (E−12)
U. S. Department of State: 85 (A−9); 98 (H−6); 103 (L−13); 121 (P−29)

Valdes, Nelson P.: 142 (T−14)
Vandenbroucke, Lucien S.: 127 (Q−33)
Van DeMark, Brian: 142 (T−15)
Varney, Harold L.: 90 (B−25)

Walton, Richard: 107 (M−17)
Waltz, Kenneth: 132 (R−37)
Wedge, Bryant: 114 (N−9)
Weintal, Edward: 86 (A−10)
Welch, Richard E., Jr.: 113 (M−63); 125 (Q−22)
West, Thomas R.: 106 (M−1)
White, Theodore: 91 (C−7)
Wicker, Tom: 91 (C−8)
Wilcox, Francis O.: 98 (H−5)
Wiles, P.: 114 (N−1)
Williams, William A.: 125 (Q−23)
Wohlstetter, Albert: 132 (R−37)
Wohlstetter, Roberta: 95 (E−13); 132 (R−37)
Wolfe, Thomas W.: 119 (P−16)
Wyden, Peter: 127 (Q−34)

Young, Oran R.: 129 (R−16)
Yarmolinsky, Adam: 113 (M−64)
York, Herbert F.: 93 (D−9)

Zorin, Valerian A.: 103 (L−18)